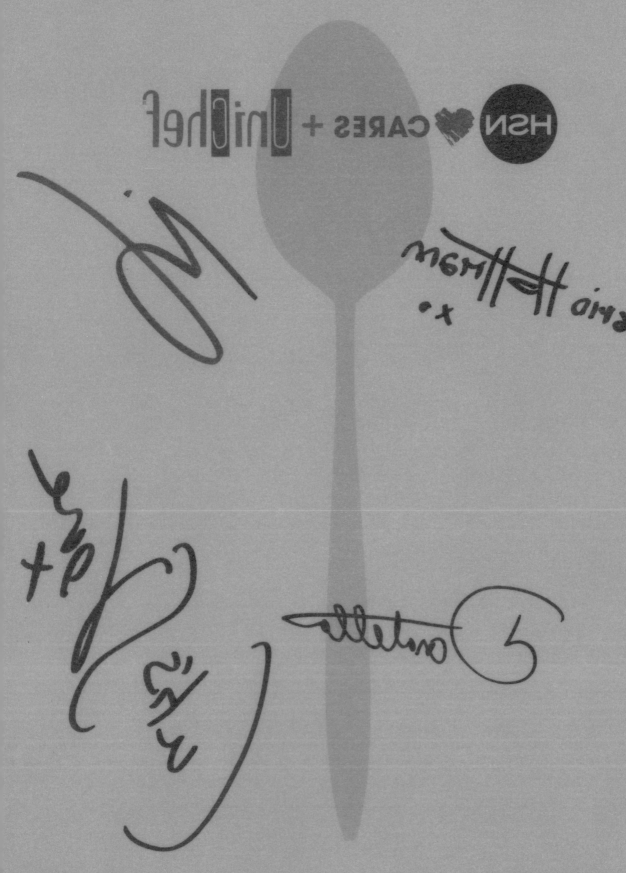

UniChef™

First published in 2014 by

INCORPORATED

New York | London

New York Office:
322 West 57th Street #19T, New York, New York 10019
Telephone: 212 362 9119

London Office:
1 Rona Road, London NW3 2HY
Tel/Fax +44 (0) 207 267 9739

www.GlitteratiIncorporated.com
media@GlitteratiIncorporated.com for inquiries

First edition, 2014

Library of Congress Cataloging-in-Publication Data
is available from the Publisher.

Hardcover First Edition 978-0-9913419-5-5
HSN Edition 978-0-9903808-0-1

Design: Sarah Morgan Karp/smk-design.com

Reprographics by Studio Fasoli, Italy
Printed in China by CP Printing Limited

10 9 8 7 6 5 4 3 2 1

Top Chefs Unite
— in Support of —
The World's Children

UniChef ™

Hilary Gumbel

with Kate Meyers & Scott Mowbray

Foreword by Danny Kaye

Glitterati
INCORPORATED

New York | London

CONTENTS

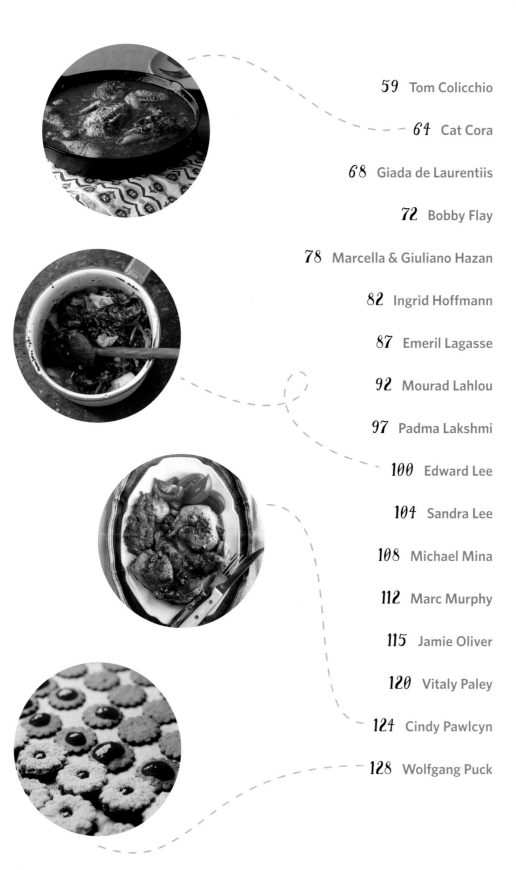

FOREWORD

"Children are the world's most valuable natural resource."

–Danny Kaye

These eloquent words of UNICEF's first Goodwill Ambassador, Danny Kaye, spoken during his lifetime, have been generously woven together by his daughter, Dena Kaye, and demonstrate all of the special merits for which UNICEF continues to stand.

I've been fortunate enough to have had many roles in my profession—actor, singer, dancer, comedian—and, thanks to UNICEF, I've also had the opportunity to be a friend to children around the world. When I was first invited to come by the UNICEF offices, I didn't realize at the time that UNICEF would capture my heart and define a large part of my life.

When I learned about all that UNICEF was doing to help the world's less fortunate children, I knew I had to go out and see for myself. It was incredible to watch the plans developed by people from 26 nations around a table at the United Nations in New York put into practice. And I wasn't the only one who was eager to see what was going on. When I was on-site in India helping dispense vaccinations for tuberculosis, everybody and his cow came to see what the fuss was about. Something very special was happening. You could feel it.

In my travels I saw so many children who should have been running and playing and enjoying their youth but were instead suffering from disease and malnutrition. It was difficult to witness, but the looks in those children's eyes kept us pushing on. I have to admit, I've always been a sucker for kids. The best applause I ever got was alongside lines of children waiting to be inoculated. I may not be a doctor, but I do have a talent for making funny faces. Without these shots, many of the babies would have died before they were 5 years old. But for one nickel, five cents, the cost of one BCG vaccination (the TB vaccination), they were given an 80% chance to live. Malaria, malnutrition, tuberculosis—you name it and you could find it. So if you got a smile you were that much ahead of the game.

I also saw incredible changes and positive transformation, not just in kids' physical health but also in their spirits. The luckier kids, the ones who responded well to their treatments, played sports and games to restore their strength. Sometimes the best exercise was as simple as bending down to pick some flowers. That's when you knew they were feeling better, when they could stop to enjoy the beauty around them. Their happy laughter came courtesy of UNICEF.

I now understand the literal meaning of the initials that make up UNICEF: *United Nations International Children's Emergency Fund.* But in fact they stand for so much more than that: compassion, generosity, and a willingness to see beyond differences in culture and circumstance. To sum it up, UNICEF is committed to the belief that the happiness all children deserve begins with better health. To me, there's nothing simpler or more important. Every kid has a right to be happy. You can help with candy and clowning, but unless a child has a future that offers a chance to grow up healthy, candy and clowning are only part-time remedies.

One of the most important things UNICEF does is bring clean, nutritious meals to hungry children. I've always loved being in the kitchen with friends because food has power to bring people together.

There's a wonderful intimacy that comes from sharing a meal with others. This basic sense of human connection was so evident to me when I saw kids who were finally getting much needed meals. When they wanted seconds, they'd say, "May I please have some more UNICEF?"

Danny Kaye
Circa 1956

Danny Kaye (1911-1987) was a virtuoso entertainer, honored with Oscars, Emmys, Peabodys, Golden Globes, the French Legion of Honor, and the Presidential Medal of Freedom.

Kaye was appointed UNICEF's first Goodwill Ambassador to the world's children in 1954, a post he cherished until the end of his life. He was the role model for future generations of celebrities worldwide who would undertake the support of a charity. He received two honorary Oscars for his humanitarian work, including the Jean Hersholt Humanitarian Award in 1982. In 1965, he joined UNICEF's official delegation in Oslo, Norway, when the organization received the Nobel Peace Prize.

In 1979, Kaye celebrated his 25th anniversary as UNICEF's first Goodwill Ambassador and made *The Guinness Book of Records* by piloting a private jet to 65 cities in the U.S. and Canada in five days, stopping at each city's airport to greet huge crowds of UNICEF volunteers for Halloween's Trick-or-Treat campaign.

When Kaye died on March 3, 1987, he not only stood for excellence in his profession but had reached a level of intellectual, artistic and humanitarian achievement attained by few.

His daughter, Dena Kaye, heads the Danny Kaye and Sylvia Fine Kaye Foundation, which continues to honor her father's legacy by having made grants to such projects as the Danny Kaye Theatre at the Culinary Institute of America. She continues to be an active member of the UNICEF family.

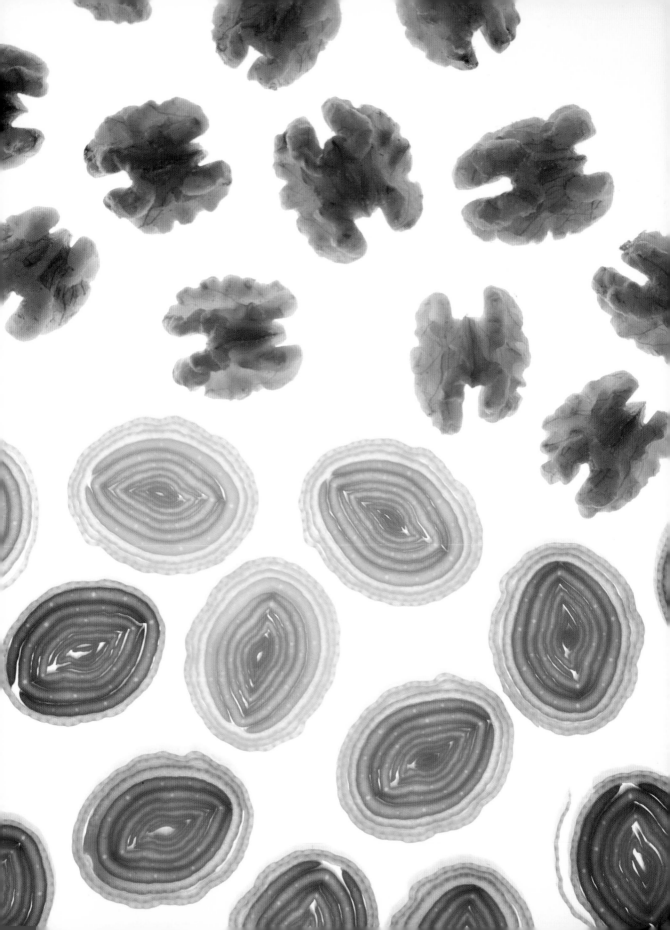

PREFACE

There are certain foods that immediately transport me to places from my past—places filled with happy memories and special moments shared with people I love. One whiff of butter cookies baking in an oven, and I am perched on a stepstool beside the stove, an apron matching the one my mom is wearing tied twice around my waist, learning how to bake on a rainy Saturday afternoon. Or, at the sight of poppy seeds mixed with sugar, I am in Sag Harbor, seated at my aunt's table, my legs still sandy from the beach, getting ready to dig into a *Zwetschgenknoedel*—a kind of Austrian plum dumpling rolled in the poppy seed mixture. Freshly made, piping hot, sweet tomato-rice soup mixed with the smells of a brisket in the oven, and I am once again listening to my grandmother assign seats at her table in the Bronx as we prepare for Shabbat dinner. And chocolate—well, chocolate, I am at my friend Barbara's house and I've just broken up with a boyfriend.

We nurture with food; we pass on traditions with food; we celebrate with food; we heal with food.

But I have also seen what happens when there is no food—when a mom is forced to choose which child to feed and which to send to bed without eating, or left with no choice but to watch the light usually shining in her child's eyes begin to fade from hunger, or worse, go out altogether. In many of the developing nations I have visited through my work on behalf of the world's children, I have seen the horrors of malnutrition, of extreme food shortages, of periods of famine during particularly dry seasons. I have encountered mothers wandering through barren desserts in search of anything edible and those who have stood in long lines in the wake of a natural disaster, hoping for something that will sustain their families.

I have also seen what happens when people care, when they reach out to help children whom they will never meet, whose bellies are empty or who have other needs equally unmet, children denied the childhood that every child deserves—people who understand that children do not choose the country or economic circumstances into which they are born.

The author of this book, Hilary Gumbel, is such a person. A longtime UNICEF volunteer and supporter, Hilary has crossed the globe on behalf of the world's children, raising resources and advocating on their behalf.

Hilary, along with each chef who contributed to this book, reminds us of the joys of cooking—of having food bring us together and unite us in ways that extend beyond just breaking bread. By taking part in this project, they are making it possible for children around the globe to share in that joy. No greater gift can be given.

Caryl M. Stern
President and Chief Executive Officer
The U.S. Fund for UNICEF

INTRODUCTION

To sit across from a 5-year-old child in a remote village in the hills of the Lamay District of Peru on a UNICEF field visit is to realize how endlessly different human beings from different parts of the world can be. But to share a quinoa cookie, packed with nutritional value, with that same child is to have an instant feeling of how alike we actually are. That connection is one that doesn't require translation; it bridges the divide between cultural differences. It is the common language of food, the joy of taste, and a shared smile that any face from anywhere can understand. It is this sense of connection, shared throughout the world, that provided the inspiration for this cookbook.

Each chef who contributed to this book said yes, because it meant they were going to be helping to provide children and their families with the means to a better life. In reaching out to a list of the world's most diverse and celebrated chefs, I had only to explain that my goal was to maximize the strength and visibility they could bring to UNICEF's mission of helping others. Each chef generously donated recipes, photographs, and time in an effort to build this mosaic volume of traditions, tastes, foods, and cultural values.

Over the past eight years, I have had the opportunity to see UNICEF's work in many different countries— Vietnam, Angola, Haiti, Peru, Uruguay, and, most recently, Senegal. Each field visit gave me the chance to see firsthand the scope of UNICEF's work and the extent to which children and families are positively impacted by that work.

UNICEF doesn't swoop in and put a Band-Aid on a problem. Instead, they offer solutions that empower families to improve and to thrive. Whether it is a 5-year-old learning the importance of nutrition in Peru, or a child in Angola excited to have new school supplies, there are many positive stories to be found amidst the magnitude of global poverty.

Because of UNICEF, we can imagine the day when zero children die from preventable diseases, when zero children lack access to basic education, and when zero children suffer from lack of clean water or basic nutrition.

By purchasing this book, you are helping provide solutions that will make a permanent difference in the world, and your support will inspire others to do the same. I thank you.

www.unicef.org

Hilary Gumbel

If you want to go fast, go alone.
If you want to go far, go together.

African proverb

Hugh Acheson

Empire State South / Atlanta

Hugh Acheson is a poster child of culinary cultural cross-pollination: a Canadian who has found his home and made his chef's bones in the American South.

Acheson's parents divorced when he was young and, with the exception of a few years he spent living with his mother and stepfather in Clemson, South Carolina, and Atlanta, Georgia, he and his three older sisters were raised by their father in Ottawa.

"I can remember being very interested in food seasonality early," he told Anna Lanfreschi of HLN. "It was very vivid to me what seasons meant in Canada, where I grew up. Corn season was a very specific two-week period, and then raspberry season. Before that you had tomatoes, and before that you had strawberries. I think that's when you get very passionate, waiting for great food to appear on the scene."

Acheson started working in restaurants after school and on weekends. His training included stints with Rob MacDonald in Canada, as well as Mike Fennelly and Gary Danko in San Francisco. It was in Georgia, however, that he developed his cooking style, a hybrid of Southern and European. He had lived in Athens, Georgia, while his wife was attending graduate school, and returned to open his first restaurant, Five & Ten, in March 2000. In 2007 he and fellow chef Peter Dale opened The National, also in Athens. In 2010 he expanded to Atlanta, opening Empire State South. The latter offers Acheson's boldest, most playful menu, with dishes such as Boiled Peanut Hummus, and Fall Lettuces and Beets with Radish, Smoked Croutons, and Georgia Olive Oil.

Acheson, like many from the North, has a keen feeling for the traditions of his new home. "I think the artisan food movement has made us look more closely at what we've lost," he told Coca-Cola's online magazine *Journey*. "The idea that the kid down the street, the 18-year-old in the sorority house, has no idea what their grandmother did with scuppernongs. When we lose that, that's when we lose the beauty of foods. Foods are now made to be so easy. But beauty is not easy."

The James Beard 2012 winner for Best Chef: Southeast published his first cookbook, *A New Turn in the South,* in 2011. He has been a fixture on Bravo's *Top Chef,* where he first competed and later served as a judge.

Chef Hugh Acheson's

FALL SALAD of CAULIFLOWER, BUTTER LETTUCE, BRUSSELS, RADISH, CURRANTS & CARROT WITH CIDER VINAIGRETTE

I love vegetables. I also think the world needs to embrace the salad bowl instead of yearning for all of our fast-food mistakes. We will change the way kids eat by showing them the bounty of vegetables early in life, by making them aware of the beauty of the radish when they are 2 years old, not 12. By 12 it's too late and they have shaped their likes and dislikes. You may get them back onto the vegetable trail later in life, maybe after college when they dine with a date or a boss and have to eat fancy vegetables, but to me that means a waste of the first 20 years. We change the world by teaching them how to make salad. Period. It's going to be awesome.

Cider Vinaigrette:

1 cup nonalcoholic apple cider (240 mL), reduced to ¼ cup (60 mL) over medium heat

1 tablespoon cider vinegar (15 mL)

1 tablespoon freshly squeezed lemon juice (15 mL)

1 teaspoon grain mustard (5 mL)

1 teaspoon chopped fresh flat-leaf parsley (5 mL)

3 tablespoons grapeseed oil (45 mL)

¼ teaspoon kosher salt (1 mL)

Freshly ground black pepper to taste

Salad:

2 cups small cauliflower florets (215 g)

1 teaspoon olive oil (5 mL)

¼ teaspoon kosher salt (1 mL)

1 cup Brussels sprout leaves, blanched (90 g)

1 head butter lettuce, cored

½ cup thinly sliced radishes (60 g)

½ cup thinly sliced young carrots (70 g)

½ cup dried currants (70 g)

1 To prepare the vinaigrette, combine the reduced cider, cider vinegar, lemon juice, mustard, parsley, grapeseed oil, salt, and as much pepper as you like in a mason jar, cap securely, and shake vigorously to blend. Slowly drizzle in the grapeseed oil to emulsify. Season with salt and pepper.

2 Preheat the oven to 450° (230°C).

3 To prepare the salad, place the cauliflower florets in a large cast-iron skillet and season with 1 teaspoon olive oil (5 mL) and ¼ teaspoon kosher salt (1 mL). Roast the cauliflower florets at 450° (230°C) for 12 minutes. Transfer the cauliflower to a plate, and let cool.

4 In a large salad bowl, arrange the cauliflower, Brussels sprout leaves, lettuces, radishes, and carrots, keeping each ingredient somewhat separated from the others. Sprinkle the salad with the currants, and serve the well-shaken vinaigrette, still in the mason jar, with the dish, so guests can dress as they like.

José Andrés

Oyamel / Washington, DC

Tireless, talkative, passionate, generous, hilarious—these are a few of the adjectives used to describe the Spanish chef and personality that is José Andrés. No less force than Anthony Bourdain has weighed in on the magnitude of Andrés's personality: "Anywhere he goes, whether he's ever been there or not, it doesn't matter: He's the mayor."

Born in 1969 in Mieres, Spain, Andrés began cooking by helping his mother bake. By 12, he was tackling paella; by 16 he was studying at a renowned culinary academy. While there, Andrés acquired practical experience apprenticing at elBulli under chef and mentor Ferran Adrià, the magician-engineer of molecular cuisine.

Andrés came to the U.S. in his early twenties and eventually landed in Washington, D.C., where he headed up the kitchen at Jaleo, helping to create one of the first critically and commercially successful tapas restaurants in the country. In 2003, with the opening of his minibar by José Andrés, the *New York Times* hailed him as "the boy wonder of culinary Washington." He has, of course, cooked at the White House.

"To me, [cooking] is so much more than work or what pays my salary," he says in his book *Tapas: A Taste of Spain in America.* "As I've traveled across America, I've learned so much about this country's cooking and so much more about my own country's cooking. I'm absorbed by the search for what happened through the centuries—the different cultures, religions, and peoples that shaped Spanish cooking into what it is today. It was only by exploring the New World that I could see the real nature of the Old."

Andrés has created more than a dozen restaurants, from the chic L.A. Bazaar to China Poblano, a Mexican-Chinese restaurant in Las Vegas, to the modern urban Oyamel, serving Mexican small plates in his home base of Washington, D.C.. His long list of honors includes the 2001 James Beard Award for Outstanding Chef. He has TV shows in the U.S., Spain, and Latin America, and he has a teaching gig at Harvard.

He is chairman emeritus for DC Central Kitchen, an organization that combats hunger and creates opportunities with culinary training. His most recent food advocacy project is the World Central Kitchen, an organization he founded after traveling to post-earthquake Haiti. Its mission: "to feed and empower vulnerable people in humanitarian crises around the world."

Chef José Andrés's

HUEVOS A LA CUBANA

When I was a young boy in Spain, I remember watching both of my parents cook. We rarely went to restaurants because we didn't always have the money. So cooking was always a great part of our family. I remember that at the beginning of the month, when we had a little bit more money, we would cook more meats. But later in the month, we would get more vegetables, cheeses, and eggs from the markets and create more humble dishes. Funny enough, the end of the month was my favorite time of all. These were the dishes that were comforting to me. Huevos a la Cubana has been one of my favorite dishes since I was a child. It is a humble dish with simple ingredients: rice, tomato, and eggs. These are the type of dishes that make me appreciate the goodness of the earth. It is amazing how you can come up with some of the most astonishing creations just by incorporating these basic foods.

1 cup plus 1½ tablespoons
extra-virgin olive oil (262 ml)

2 garlic cloves, smashed and peeled

1 cup Bomba rice (200 g)
or other short-grain rice

2 cups mineral water (480 ml)

Salt to taste

Tomato Sauce (recipe follows)

½ pound bacon (about 10 slices) (240 g)

1 banana

4 large eggs

Fresh tarragon (optional)

1. To prepare the rice, heat 1 tablespoon olive oil (15 ml) in a medium sauté pan over medium-high heat. Add 2 garlic cloves, and sauté until very lightly browned, about 1 to 2 minutes.

2. Add the rice to the pan, and stir with a wooden spoon, ensuring every grain is coated with oil. Add mineral water, and season with salt. Reduce the heat, and simmer, stirring occasionally, until all the water has evaporated and the rice is almost cooked through (about 15 minutes). Spread the rice on a baking sheet to cool.

3. Meanwhile, warm the Tomato Sauce in a small saucepan over medium-low heat. While warming the tomato sauce, cook the bacon in a medium frying pan over medium-high heat until crispy. Transfer bacon to a paper towel–lined plate, and keep warm. Peel the banana and cut in half. Slice the 2 halves lengthwise, so you have 4 pieces. In the same frying pan, sear the banana pieces, about 15 to 20 seconds on each side. Transfer to the plate with the bacon, and keep warm.

4. In a separate small sauté pan, heat 1 cup olive oil (240 ml) over high heat to about 375° (190°C) (measured with a candy thermometer). Crack an egg into a small glass, and season with salt. Tip the sauté pan to a steep angle so the oil collects on 1 side to create a small bath. Carefully slide the egg into the hot oil. Using a wooden spoon, ladle the oil over the egg 2 or 3 times, cooking until golden brown. The egg will be ready in just 30 seconds. Using a slotted spoon, transfer the egg to a warm plate lined with paper towels to absorb the excess oil. Repeat with the remaining eggs.

5. In the same sauté pan used to prepare the rice, heat the remaining ½ tablespoon olive oil (7 ml) over medium-high heat. Allow the pan to get hot; then return the rice to the pan, and sauté for about 2 minutes.

6. To serve, spread about ¼ cup of the warmed Tomato Sauce (60 ml) onto a plate. Spoon about ½ cup rice (100 g) over the tomato sauce, and top with a fried egg. Garnish with a couple of bacon slices, 1 banana piece, and fresh tarragon, if desired. Serve immediately.

1 tablespoon extra-virgin olive oil (15 mL)

¼ Spanish onion, diced

¼ green bell pepper, diced

2 garlic cloves, smashed and peeled

1 (28-ounce) can whole peeled tomatoes (794 g)

Tomato Sauce

1 To prepare the tomato sauce, in a medium saucepan, heat the oil over medium heat, and sauté the onions, bell peppers, and 2 garlic cloves until soft. Add the can of tomatoes; crush them with a wooden spoon. Over low heat, simmer the tomatoes until most of the liquid is evaporated and the tomatoes are a nice deep red. Transfer all to a blender, and puree until smooth. Set aside until ready to use.

Donatella Arpaia

Donatella Pizzeria / New York

"Food is a part of my culture and my soul," Arpaia told *The Journal.* "When I became an adult, I realized that was what I wanted to do and what was going to make me happy."

Part of that realization came from her childhood: Arpaia grew up spending her summers in Naples and Puglia, where she loved watching her relatives pressing olives for olive oil, preserving vegetables, jarring tomato sauce, and making fresh pasta by hand. She brought her Italian memories to life in 1998 by convincing her dad to join her in opening her first restaurant, Bellini, attending the French Culinary Institute when she wasn't working.

Arpaia has always been a stylish figure in the New York food world, but as she wrote in the introduction to her 2010 cookbook, *Donatella Cooks: Simple Food Made Glamorous,* "Behind my Dior shades is a soul deeply attached to the lives of my Apulian and Neapolitan relatives. At home, my cooking style is very much indebted to the summers I spent on my grandmother's farm in Toritto in Puglia. There, in the orchards, gardens, and kitchens of my six aunts, my food sensibility was formed. Not a single one of the sisters was what you would call glamorous—think housedress and slippers for a more accurate visual—but they were using the freshest ingredients and preparing them simply, and those are the keys to becoming a good cook no matter who you are (or what you wear)."

Arpaia's celebrated list of New York City restaurants includes Donatella Pizzeria, DBar, and Kefi. A Food Network fixture, Arpaia is head judge on both *Iron Chef America* and *The Next Iron Chef.*

Donatella Arpaia first experienced the fast-paced world of a restaurant kitchen as a babe. "My crib was next to the dishwashing station of my father's first restaurant," Arpaia said in a 2013 interview with *The Journal.* Later she and her siblings worked the coat check at the family's Long Island eatery. But Arpaia's father, an emigrant from Italy who became a successful restaurateur, had bigger things in mind for his children. Like a good daughter, Arpaia set out to climb corporate ladders: She attended law school. Soon after joining a firm, however, she realized she was dealing with the wrong sort of torts.

4 medium zucchini, finely diced

2 eggs, lightly beaten

2 tablespoons chopped fresh
flat-leaf parsley (30 mL)

½ cup grated Parmigiano-Reggiano
cheese (50 g)

1 teaspoon extra-virgin olive oil (5 mL)

Kosher salt

Freshly ground black pepper

¾ to 1 cup all-purpose flour (94 g to 125 g)

Olive oil

Chef Donatella Arpaia's

ZUCCHINI FRITTERS

One bite of these fritters, and I'm taken back to my Long Island grade school. Instead of packing PB&J in a Farrah Fawcett lunch box, my mother sent me off with foil-wrapped fritters stuffed into a brown paper bag. Despite the fact that I whined for a more mainstream lunch and was relentlessly picked on, I secretly loved these! Today, I beg my mother to make them. Hers are without question the best, but mine are a pretty close second. She never grates the zucchini (which I am always tempted to do because it's quicker—alas, results in a watery batter), but rather cuts the zucchini into almost confetti-like pieces. The tinier the zucchini pieces, the better. Use a food processor with the fine-dice attachment for best results, or cut by hand the way my mommy does it.

1 Combine the zucchini, eggs, parsley, Parmigiano, and extra-virgin olive oil; stir until the zucchini is coated. Season generously with salt and pepper. Add ¾ cup flour (94 g), a sprinkle at a time, and stir. Continue adding until the mixture is the consistency of pancake batter. Add more if the zucchini is very wet.

2 Fill a large, heavy-bottomed pan with ¼ inch olive oil (6 mm). Heat over medium heat until hot but not smoking. Working in batches, spoon the zucchini mixture into the pan in 2-tablespoon mounds (30 ml). The fritters should be three-quarters submerged in the oil. If bits of zucchini stray, scoop them up and return them to the fritters. Reduce the heat slightly, and fry until golden brown, turning once, about 5 minutes per side. Remove from the pan with a slotted spoon, and drain on paper towels. Allow the oil to return to medium heat before proceeding with the next batch. Serve the fritters on a parchment-lined tray. The leftover fritters will keep, covered and refrigerated, up to 2 days. Reheat, wrapped in foil, in a low oven.

Mario Batali

Babbo / New York

Mario Batali's infectious exuberance, married with a reverence for the authentic, has made him one of America's most beloved and successful chefs of Italian food. Whether in the inner sanctum of his original Manhattan restaurant, Babbo; in the high-toned culinary temple of Del Posto; or at a counter seat at his vegetarian mini-restaurant in the Eataly food hall, the Batali trademarks are deep flavor and an absence of fussiness, no matter how complex the dish.

This he famously learned from his grandmother Leonetta Merlino in Seattle, who made dishes like hand-rolled ravioli stuffed with calf's brains, pork sausage, Swiss chard, and cheese.

Oddly, Batali once imagined himself a Spanish financier, his family having lived in Spain and his college majors at Rutgers having been business management and Spanish theater. He was wooed into the culinary life while working and partying in equal measure at a pizza restaurant elegantly called Stuff Yer Face. After college, Batali went to London's Cordon Bleu school but soon dropped out. He then worked for Marco Pierre White, a chef known for his Michelin triumphs and thundering, theatrical temper. Batali cooked professionally in the United States in the 1980s but did not find his calling until he moved to Italy to pursue authentic Italian cuisine in his grandmother's style. In 1989, he arrived at a small train station in an Italian town, armed with his guitar and golf clubs, promising to work for room and board at a hillside restaurant called La Volta, located between Bologna and Florence.

"It was a great rush," Batali told *The New Yorker*. "I knew that first week, once I saw the food, that I'd made the right move. The food was traditional. Very simple. No sauces, no steam tables, no pans of stock, none of the things I'd learned to do. This was exactly what I'd hoped for."

He spent three years in Italy, soaking it all in, before returning to America to build an empire. Today Batali, with business partner Joe Bastianich, manages a remarkable collection of restaurants in New York, across the U.S., and internationally. He also co-owns Eataly, the multirestaurant Italian food halls in New York City and Chicago. Batali is the author of many cookbooks, a longtime TV star, and co-host of *The Chew*.

Chef Mario Batali's

BUCATINI all'AMATRICIANA

This dish is named for the town of Amatrice (about an hour east of Rome), considered by many Italians to be the birthplace of the best cooks on the peninsula.

The simplicity and deliciousness of this dish, to me, sing of everything perfect about Italian cooking. My grandmother used to make it for us when we were young. Later on as a young adult, traveling to Italy for the first time, I tasted it in a small, understated trattoria outside Rome. It felt like home, and suddenly everything came full circle.

2 tablespoons salt (30 ml)

¾ pound guanciale or pancetta, thinly sliced (360 g)

3 garlic cloves

1 red onion, halved and cut into ½-inch-thick slices (13 mm=)

1½ teaspoons crushed red pepper (7 ml)

Kosher salt and freshly ground black pepper to taste

1½ cups Basic Tomato Sauce (360 ml) (recipe follows)

1 pound bucatini pasta (480 g)

1 bunch fresh flat-leaf parsley, leaves only

Pecorino Romano cheese, for grating

1. Bring 6 quarts (5.7 L) of water to a boil, and add 2 tablespoons (30 ml) of salt.

2. Place the guanciale slices in a 12- to 14-inch (30 to 35 cm) sauté pan in a single layer, and cook over medium-low heat until most of the fat has been rendered from the meat, turning occasionally. Remove the meat to a plate lined with paper towels, and discard half the fat, leaving enough to coat the garlic, onion, and crushed red pepper. Return the guanciale to the pan with the onion, garlic, and red pepper, and cook over medium-high heat for 5 minutes or until the onions, garlic, and guanciale are light golden brown. Season with salt and pepper, add the tomato sauce, reduce the heat, and simmer for 10 minutes.

3. Cook the bucatini in the boiling water according to the package directions, until al dente. Drain the pasta, and add it to the simmering sauce. Add the parsley leaves, and increase the heat to high; toss to coat. Divide the pasta among 4 warmed pasta bowls. Top with freshly grated Pecorino Romano cheese, and serve immediately.

¼ cup extra-virgin olive oil (60 ml)

1 Spanish onion, cut in ¼-inch dice (6 mm)

4 garlic cloves, peeled and thinly sliced

3 tablespoons chopped fresh thyme leaves (9 g/45 ml) or 1 tablespoon dried (15 ml)

½ medium carrot, finely shredded

2 (28-ounce) cans peeled whole tomatoes, (2 [794-g] cans) crushed by hand and juices reserved

Salt to taste

Basic Tomato Sauce

1. In a 3-quart (2.8 L) saucepan, heat the olive oil over medium heat. Add the onion and garlic, and cook until soft and light golden brown, about 8 to 10 minutes. Add the thyme and carrot, and cook 5 minutes more, until the carrot is quite soft. Add the tomatoes and juice, and bring to a boil, stirring often. Lower the heat, and simmer for 30 minutes until as thick as hot cereal. Season with salt, and serve. This sauce holds 1 week in the refrigerator or up to 6 months in the freezer.

Yield: 4 cups (960 ml)

Paul Berglund

The Bachelor Farmer / Minneapolis

When The Bachelor Farmer opened in the heart of Nordic-American country in 2011, it proved there was a market for a modern interpretation of local culinary heritage. Scandinavian immigrants had been coming to the Midwest since the late 1800s, finding the landscape familiar (and, in winter, a bit kinder), ideal for their traditions of dairy farming, curing and smoking fish, and foraging for mushrooms and bitter greens. In the region, Scandinavian heritage became a local reference point, even a joke on Garrison Keillor's *A Prairie Home Companion.* Yet when Paul Berglund started as chef in Minneapolis, actual Scandinavian cooking had become an afterthought for many, or an import: Cue the Swedish meatballs at the Twin Cities Ikea café.

As befits the migratory habits of American chefs, Berglund was raised not in Minneapolis but in St. Louis, by Swedish-American parents. He attended the University of Michigan and served four years as a junior naval officer before entering the kitchen, first at Oliveto in Oakland, California. Seven years later, he started as executive chef at The Bachelor Farmer with owners Andrew and Eric Dayton (sons of Minnesota governor Mark Dayton). The menu is a deft mix of traditional notes and modern thinking, casual yet innovative enough to attract national attention.

Toasts, or *smörgås*, anchor the menu. Fresh-baked rye bread comes to the table with an array of toppers like pork shank terrine with pickled kohlrabi, or duck liver paté with blueberry jam and tangy grain mustard. Entrées range from pheasant meatballs with whey-braised Carola potatoes to duck breast with purple-top turnips, carrots, braised radishes, and crème fraîche. Sweets are gorgeous: In fall, Berglund has served a bay leaf flan with cinnamon whipped cream and walnut *sandbakkel* (a Norwegian sugar cookie).

Berglund sources as much as he can locally. This includes house-smoked trout out of Lake Erie, house-made cheese from a nearby dairy farm, and paper-thin pickled cucumbers from farmers markets. Other produce comes from raised beds, neatly contained in plastic kiddie pools, on the roof of the restaurant.

Chef Paul Berglund's

SWEDISH PANCAKES

Growing up, some of my fondest memories of my Grandma Svea were in her kitchen, eating meatballs and Swedish pancakes. I would eat them with cinnamon, powdered sugar, and a pat of butter. Perhaps my love of sweets started in her kitchen. Perhaps it was already formed and it's what helps me remember those mornings 30 years later.

Swedish pancakes are often eaten with lingonberries (a cranberry relative) or fresh fruit for dessert. Minnesota is maple syrup country, so I enjoy them with a bit of powdered sugar and syrup. Vanilla or cardamom ice cream is a great alternative, if you'd like to serve these as a dessert.

The whole-wheat flour is not traditional, but I enjoy its nuttiness. I like to make these the night before. They develop a more complex flavor that way. A traditional cast-iron pan to cook the *plättar* [pancake] has seven small wells for silver dollar–sized pancakes. For larger pancakes, a traditional cast-iron skillet works very well.

2 tablespoons butter, plus additional butter for cooking the pancakes (28 g)

¾ cup plus 2 teaspoons all-purpose flour (99 g)

¼ cup plus 1 teaspoon whole-wheat flour (33 g)

1 tablespoon plus 1 teaspoon sugar (20 g)

½ teaspoon kosher salt (2 ml)

1¾ cups whole milk (420 ml)

3 eggs, lightly beaten

1 Melt the butter, and let cool.

2 Combine the two flours, sugar, and salt in a mesh sieve; sift into a large bowl. Combine the milk and eggs in a bowl. Add the milk mixture to the flour mixture, and whisk until incorporated. Whisk in the melted butter. Cover and refrigerate overnight. The batter should be used within 24 hours.

3 Heat a cast-iron skillet over medium-low heat. When hot, add a small amount of butter to the pan just to coat. I like to brush it on with a kitchen brush. The pan is the right temperature when the butter starts to toast lightly right away. Add enough batter to thinly cover the entire pan. Wait until you see bubbles forming in the center of the pancake. Flip it, and cook the pancake until the bottom is lightly browned. Serve immediately if you have hungry grandchildren waiting. Otherwise, store finished pancakes in a 200° (90°C) oven until you are ready to eat.

Daniel Boulud

Daniel / New York

Daniel Boulud is the most influential French chef to cook in America since Jacques Pépin: The standard-setting restaurateur defined contemporary French cooking at both the haute and the bistro level, brilliantly adapting his food to American tastes.

Boulud grew up on his family's farm in a small village outside Lyon, France. He faced a choice: work on the farm or help his grandmother, a wonderful cook, in the kitchen. The choice was easy. "I knew at 14 what real food should be," he told The Artist Toolbox. "I had real food at home because I was born on a farm, and every day we would be eating all our harvest at the table and the food was fresh, the food was beautiful. The food was very simple, very humble, but very special."

Boulud spent his formative years working in the kitchens of Michelin-starred legends Roger Vergé, Georges Blanc, and Michel Guérard. Two years in Copenhagen followed before he landed in Washington, D.C., and then New York City, where he worked at the Polo Lounge and Le Regence before a six-year stint as executive chef at Manhattan society spotlight Le Cirque. The Boulud era began with the opening of Daniel—suddenly Manhattan's most elegant dining temple—in 1993. Boulud then opened db Bistro Moderne, launching the haute burger trend with his devastatingly rich hamburger of braised short ribs, foie gras, and black truffle. He went on to build a restaurant empire that spans New York, Miami, London, Beijing, and Montréal. He's authored eight cookbooks, including DANIEL: My French Cuisine in 2013, and his culinary accolades include James Beard Awards for Outstanding Restaurateur; Best Chef: New York City; and Outstanding Chef of the Year.

Boulud's cooking is French at its core but draws on influences from the Mediterranean, India, and Japan. "I would say that the hardware is French," he told Time, "but the software can be more local and more spontaneous and certainly a combination of flavors. Even if I use Asian ingredients, I always think French balance and seasoning."

His restaurants, no matter how starred, are congenial, a trait that's simply in his bones. "For almost one hundred years," he wrote in the Café Boulud Cookbook, "the locals of St.-Pierre-de-Chandieu, my small hometown outside Lyon, met daily at the roadside Café Boulud, the petit café and not quite restaurant that my great-grandparents, grandparents, and later my parents took pride in tending on their family farm. It was the rendezvous point for generations of townsfolk. It was the place people went to begin and finish a day, to toast births and marriages, and to mourn losses. It was where love affairs started and, of course, where some ended. It was warm, welcoming, and a vital part of village life. And, it was a memory I always carried with me."

SHORT RIBS MIROTON

Miroton—a French version of an Irish stew—is a dish I can remember making with my grandmother on our family farm in Lyon when I was a very young boy. The meat would come from an animal on the farm—lamb shoulder, veal breast, short rib—and cook alongside potatoes and vegetables from the garden. It was the perfect meal for a working family, prepared early in the day while we tended to the farm and ready to serve many hungry mouths. It's a cherished memory of how food can be nourishing, nostalgic, and nationalistic.

When braising, remember to use a pot that has a tightly fitting lid, which reduces the amount of liquid needed for cooking and results in more concentrated flavors.

You can prepare this winter dish up to three hours in advance; just add extra liquid if needed and reheat 15 to 20 minutes prior to serving.

3 pounds beef short ribs (1.4 kg) (about 2 inches thick [5 cm]), cut in pairs, fat removed

1 bottle dry white wine (750 mL) (such as a Mâcon white)

½ pound onions (240 g), peeled and cut into large wedges

¼ pound bacon (120 g), cut in ½-inch cubes (13 mm)

Salt and crushed black peppercorns

2 sprigs fresh thyme

6 sprigs parsley, leaves chopped and reserved, stems set aside

1 bay leaf

2 tablespoons sweet butter (28 g)

2 tablespoons all-purpose flour (30 mL)

2 pounds medium red or white potatoes (960 g) (about the size of a lemon), scrubbed and halved

1 Marinate the short ribs in a nonreactive bowl (porcelain or stainless steel) with the white wine, onions, bacon, 1 teaspoon (5 ml) each salt and peppercorns, and a bouquet garni made of the thyme sprigs, parsley stems, and bay leaf tied together with kitchen string. Mix well, cover, and refrigerate overnight (or a minimum of 8 hours). When marinated, drain in a colander set over a bowl; reserve the marinade. Set both the drained ingredients and the marinade aside.

2 Preheat oven to 425° (220°C).

3 In a roasting pan on top of the stove, melt the butter over high heat. Add the ribs and bacon; sauté on both sides, about 10 to 12 minutes or until lightly browned. Add the marinated onions and bouquet garni, mix well, and sweat for 10 more minutes. Sprinkle with the flour, and bake at 425° (220°C) for 5 to 7 minutes. Return the roasting pan to the stove over medium heat, and toss well for 3 minutes. Add the marinade, potatoes, salt, and pepper; mix. Cover and bake at 425° (220°C) for 45 minutes to 1 hour and 15 minutes, depending on the thickness of the meat and potatoes. Mix well every 15 minutes while cooking. Remove and discard the herbs. Sprinkle chopped parsley leaves over the top. Serve the miroton in the cooking pot.

Anthony Bourdain

Author, TV Host, Producer

Chef and author Anthony Bourdain is best known for traveling the globe for his TV show *Anthony Bourdain: No Reservations.* Somewhat notoriously, he has established himself as a professional gadfly, bête noire, advocate, social critic, and pork enthusiast, recognized worldwide for his caustic sense of humor. He is as unsparing of those things he hates as he is evangelical about his passions.

The chef-at-large at New York's famed Brasserie Les Halles, Bourdain is the author of the bestselling *Kitchen Confidential: Adventures in the Culinary Underbelly*, a candid, hysterical, and sometimes shocking portrait of life in restaurant kitchens that has been translated into more than 28 languages—as well as the travel journal *A Cook's Tour,* the nonfiction *Medium Raw,* 4 crime novels, a cookbook, a biography of Typhoid Mary, the bestselling graphic novel *Get Jiro!,* and others.

His work has appeared in *The New Yorker, The New York Times, The Times* of London, *Bon Appétit, Gourmet,* and many other publications. He has shared his insights about team building and crisis management with the *Harvard Business Review.* He has been profiled by *CBS Sunday Morning* and *Nightline* and has been a guest on *Late Show with David Letterman, Morning Joe, TODAY* show, *Late Night with Jimmy Fallon, Jimmy Kimmel Live, The Daily Show with Jon Stewart, Charlie Rose, The Colbert Report,* and *Real Time with Bill Maher.*

Bourdain joined the writing staff of HBO's *Treme* in 2011, contributing to the popular drama's restaurant story lines. He recently launched his own publishing line with Ecco, Anthony Bourdain Books, an imprint of HarperCollins. The first titles were released in 2013.

Anthony Bourdain: No Reservations, which he made from 2004 to 2012, was widely popular all over the world, has won two Emmy Awards, and has garnered several other nominations. The year 2013 saw the premiere of two new television shows hosted by Bourdain: *The Taste,* a cooking competition series for ABC with Nigella Lawson, and *Parts Unknown,* a travel docu-series for CNN.

SOUPE DE POISSON

One of my first taste memories of France is of the murky, brown *soupe de poisson* they served at a shabby little café near my Tante Jeanne's house in the oyster village of La Teste. I fell in love with the stuff. The deep, dark fish broth, heavily scented with garlic and anis, the croutons I'd smear with peppery rouille and sprinkle (incongruously) with cheese. Later—much later—when I found myself cooking for a living, it was a dish, an experience, I worked hard at re-creating. It was the taste of childhood France I was trying to capture: rough, rustic, unpretentious—the very opposite of white tablecloth Paris. The key to this dish is the fish stock (do not be shy with the garlic). It should be dark, ugly, assertive—and roughly reassuring. Best served in a chipped bowl with a not particularly good *vin de table*.

If you go with the heads-and-bones option, I suggest you ask your fishmonger for the "racks," or bones and heads, of fresh red snapper or grouper or similar white-fleshed, non-oily fish. Bluefish, salmon, or mackerel will not do.

6 tablespoons olive oil (90 ml)

4 garlic cloves

2 small onions, thinly sliced

2 leeks, whites only, washed
and thinly sliced

1 fennel bulb, thinly sliced

1 (18 ounce) can plum tomatoes
(500 g), chopped

2 pounds tiny whole fish (900 g)
(like porgies or whiting), gutted but
heads intact, or 4 pounds fish bones
and heads (1.8 kg)

1 bouquet garni (a few sprigs of
fresh parsley, thyme, and a bay leaf
tied together in a bundle with natural
twine or placed in a muslin bag)

Zest of 1 orange

3 strands of saffron

Salt and pepper

1 ounce Pernod (28 ml)

Croutons

Rouille (recipe follows)

Grated Parmesan

1 In a large, heavy-bottomed pot, heat the olive oil over medium heat. Add the garlic, onions, leeks, and fennel, and let them sweat for about 5 minutes, stirring occasionally with a wooden spoon. Add the tomatoes and cook for another 4 to 5 minutes; then add the small fish or the bones. Cook for about 15 minutes, stirring occasionally. Add water to cover, as well as the bouquet garni and orange zest. Stir well; add the saffron, salt and pepper, and Pernod. Lower the heat and simmer for about an hour.

2 Remove the pot from the heat and let the soup cool slightly. Taking care not to splatter or scald yourself, strain the liquid into a large bowl. In the pot, crush the heads, bones, and vegetables as much as possible, and transfer that to a strainer over a bowl. Push and squeeze every bit of liquid and solid goodness through with a mallet or heavy wooden spoon. Return to the pot.

3 Bring the soup back up to heat, and serve with croutons, Rouille, and some grated Parmesan on the side. The idea is to smear a little Rouille on the croutons, float them in the soup as garnish, and allow guests to sprinkle cheese as they wish.

1 large garlic clove, crushed

½ red bell pepper, roasted,
peeled, and seeded

1 egg yolk

1 teaspoon freshly squeezed
lemon juice (5 mL)

Small pinch of saffron threads (0.3 mL)

1 cup extra-virgin olive oil (240 mL)

Salt

Pepper

Rouille

1 In the bowl of the food processor, combine the garlic, red pepper, egg yolk, lemon juice, and saffron. Pulse until smooth; then slowly drizzle in the oil and process continuously until the mixture thickens. Season with salt and pepper to taste, and use immediately.

Yield: approximately 1 cup (240 ml)

Anne Burrell

Secrets of a Restaurant Chef | Food Network

As a 3-year-old in upstate New York in 1972, Anne Burrell told her mother she had a friend named Julia. She was, of course, referring to Julia Child, whom she loved to watch on television.

Burrell's first kitchen job was a stint as a fry cook at McDonald's. After college, the Culinary Institute of America provided her professional training, and then she headed to Italy, where she attended the Italian Culinary Institute for Foreigners. Burrell remained in Italy for on-the-job training at restaurants in Umbria and Tuscany before moving to New York and honing her chops as a sous chef at Felidia, the restaurant owned by New York's godmother of Italian cooking, Lidia Bastianich.

"The Culinary Institute of America has a very French-based curriculum," Burrell told online magazine *Edge*. "I loved learning and knowing how to cook, but it was the Italian mentality of the ingredients and the simplicity of everything that just spoke to me."

Her next stop was Savoy, an influential early outpost of locavore thinking, where she was chef. Burrell then spent three years teaching at the Institute of Culinary Education before going back to the restaurant business and eventually joining the Batali–Bastianich empire. When Mario Batali became a Food Network Iron Chef, he chose Burrell to be his sous chef. In July 2007 Burrell was executive chef at New York's Centro Vinoteca, where she served up an Italian menu of small plates, antipasti, and pasta.

Burrell's spiky blond hair and exuberant personality made her a commanding presence alongside Batali; the camera loved her. Burrell has since appeared on several other Food Network shows, including *Secrets of a Restaurant Chef; Worst Cooks in America;* and her own competition series, *Chef Wanted,* in which candidates for executive chef restaurant jobs run the gauntlet of her blunt analyses. In 2011, her first cookbook, *Cook Like a Rock Star,* became a bestseller, and she starred in *The Next Iron Chef: Super Chefs.*

Chef Anne Burrell's

BIG BRINED HERBY TURKEY

We've all been forced to suffer through a Thanksgiving dinner with a really dry turkey, so after years of eating other people's less-than-juicy birds, I came up with a great recipe to make sure that the meat stays supersucculent. This fabulous cooking method guarantees a moist, tasty turkey. Now that I have this foolproof method down, it's become family tradition for me to make the bird. I head home to upstate New York to spend the weekend with my family ... cooking with my mom and siblings, playing with my nieces and nephews ... all that good stuff.

We all gather around in the kitchen and spend the day cooking together and preparing the Thanksgiving meal. I love showing people how to prepare this recipe, not to mention bringing together friends and family, which is a really important part of any meal—especially during the holidays.

With a three-day brine, this is definitely a think-ahead recipe.

Brine:

¾ cup kosher salt (175 g)

⅓ cup sugar (60 g)

2 onions, cut into 1/2-inch dice (13 mm)

2 carrots, cut into 1/2-inch dice (13 mm)

3 celery ribs, cut into 1/2-inch dice (13 mm)

1 whole garlic bulb, cut in half horizontally

½ bunch fresh rosemary

½ bunch fresh sage

2 tablespoons coriander seed (30 mL)

2 tablespoons fennel seed (30 mL)

6 bay leaves

1 teaspoon crushed red pepper (5 mL)

1 (15-pound) fresh turkey (6.8 kg), neck and giblets removed

Herb Butter:

½ pound (2 sticks) unsalted butter (240 g), at room temperature

½ bunch fresh rosemary, leaves finely chopped

½ bunch fresh sage, leaves finely chopped

Kosher salt

Ingredients continued on next page.

1 To brine the turkey, use a container large enough to accommodate all the ingredients including the turkey. Combine 2 gallons (7.6 L) water with the first 12 ingredients (through red pepper). Stir to combine. Submerge the turkey in the brine. Cover and refrigerate 3 days.

2 To prepare the turkey for roasting, the night before you are planning to roast the bird, remove it from the brine, and pat it dry with paper towels.

3 To prepare the herb butter, combine the butter, ½ bunch rosemary, ½ bunch sage, and some salt in a small bowl. Taste to make sure it is delicious. Using your fingers, carefully work your way under the skin of the turkey to separate it from the breasts and legs. Massage the herb butter under the skin of the breast and legs, then all over the outside of the bird as well. This will act like suntan lotion to create a lovely, crispy, brown skin. Tie the turkey's legs together with butcher's twine to create that perfect turkey shape. This will also keep the bird nice and compact for even cooking.

4 In the bottom of your roasting pan, for the gravy, combine 2 diced onions and next 5 ingredients (through 3 bay leaves). Season with salt. Plunk the turkey on top of the veggies and put it in the fridge overnight, uncovered. Yes, that's right , uncovered. This allows the skin of the turkey to dry out and creates a gorgeous, brown, crispy skin. Now a bunch of your prep work is out of the way, so all you have to do tomorrow is toss the turkey in the oven.

5 Preheat the oven to 450° (230°C).

Gravy:

2 onions, cut into ½-inch dice (13 mm)

2 carrots, cut into ½-inch dice (13 mm)

2 celery ribs, cut into ½-inch dice (13 mm)

4 garlic cloves, smashed

1 thyme bundle

3 bay leaves

2 quarts chicken stock (1.9 L)

¾ cup all-purpose flour (94 g)

2 cups dry white wine (480 mL)

6 Pour 2 cups chicken stock (480 ml) into the roasting pan, and put the turkey in the screaming hot oven for 35 to 40 minutes or until the turkey becomes beautifully browned. Reduce the heat to 350° (180°C). Baste the turkey with the pan juices, and rotate the pan every 30 minutes for the remainder of the cooking time. Think 17 minutes per pound ... you do the math. If the turkey starts to get too brown, tent it loosely with aluminum foil.

7 Remove the turkey from the oven when an instant-read thermometer registers 155° (70°C) when inserted into the thickest part of the turkey (be sure the thermometer is not touching a bone or you'll get an inaccurate reading). Transfer your beautiful bird to a rimmed baking sheet, cover loosely with aluminum foil, and let rest for at least 30 minutes.

8 To make the gravy, strain the cooking liquid in a mesh strainer over a large bowl; discard the veggies. Allow the fat to rise to the top of the cooking liquid. Save the roasting pan, but don't wash it—you still need it. Skim the fat off the surface of the cooking liquid. Place the roasting pan directly on a burner, add the skimmed fat to the pan, and bring it to medium heat. Whisk in the flour, and cook the mixture until it has the consistency of wet sand. Whisk in the wine, and cook 4 to 5 minutes. Add the reserved cooking juices and the remaining 6 cups chicken stock (1.4 L) to the flour mixture. Bring the liquid to a boil, and reduce to a simmer.

9 Cook until the mixture is the consistency of thick gravy, about 10 minutes. Taste and season with salt if needed. Carve the turkey, and serve with the gravy.

David Chang

Momofuku / New York

David Chang epitomizes a multiethnic, modern cooking style that is at once daring, loose, precise, and true, and he attained world fame bringing that style to table. Chang's disciplined-kitchen-cowboy approach and media-darling chops have inspired a whole generation of young American chefs.

Son of Korean restaurant owners, Chang was fascinated by the workings of his father's kitchen at an early age, but his father, like many immigrants, worked 30 years in a hot, hard business so that his son would never have to. "I could have chosen to be a garbage man and he would have been more pleased with the decision I'd made," he quipped at a 2009 Google talk in New York.

Cooking was not Chang's first path: He majored in religion at Trinity College in Hartford, Connecticut, and then went to Japan to teach English. There, a lifelong love of noodles turned into an all-out ramen obsession, prompting Chang to return to the States to study cooking at the French Culinary Institute in New York.

"Cooking was one of the few things that I thought was an honest craft," he told the Google audience, "that you could apply yourself and get better every day. It was remarkable because you could use your hands. You could act like a total buffoon ... there's this total chaos ... but it was under this umbrella of this French system of a brigade. I felt like I found my calling and I could do this."

The Virginia native cut his teeth in Manhattan, working for a who's who of star chefs—Jean-Georges Vongerichten, Tom Colicchio, Daniel Boulud—before opening the first of his New York restaurants, Momofuku Noodle Bar, in 2004. This was followed by Momofuku Ssäm Bar; the dessert-focused Milk Bar; and the tiny, virtuoso Momofuku Ko, whose opening in 2008 introduced diners to dishes like kimchi consommé with Malpeque oyster, pork belly, and braised cabbage; shaved foie gras over lychees, lychee gelée, and pine nut brittle; and miso soup and lard-grilled rice cake over pickled turnips and cabbage. Chang opened Má Pêche in midtown Manhattan in 2010. He currently has 11 restaurants in New York, Sydney, and Toronto. Chang's *Momofuku* cookbook came out in 2009, and his quarterly food journal, *Lucky Peach*, debuted in 2011.

Chang has been one of *Time*'s 100 most influential people (2010) and one of *GQ*'s Men of the Year (2007) and has received four James Beard Awards, including Rising Star Chef.

FUJI APPLE SALAD KIMCHI, SMOKED JOWL & MAPLE LABNE

We obviously use kimchi as often as we can at Momofuku—from kimchi sauce with our *bo ssäm* to our version of a Bloody Mary. I grew up eating kimchi with my family, and it will always be on our menus in some form. Using it with apples seemed like a crazy idea at first, but the funkiness of the kimchi pairs perfectly with the sweetness of apples.

I know, I know, there are like three leaves on the salad in the photo, but that was just to make it look pretty.

4 Fuji apples, peeled

½ cup napa cabbage kimchi, pureed (120 mL)

½ cup labne, or more to taste (120 g)

¼ cup maple syrup, or more to taste (60 mL

1 pound sliced country jowl (480 g)
from Burgers' Smokehouse or thick-cut
smoky bacon

1 loosely packed cup arugula (20 g)

2 tablespoons olive oil (30 mL)

Kosher salt

Freshly ground black pepper

1 Cut the apples into wedges or very large cubes: The size of the apples will dictate what works best—what you want are pieces that are 1 big bite or 2 small bites. If they're too thin or small, they'll be limp and won't assert their appleness; if they're too big, they won't take on enough kimchi flavor and the salad will be hard to eat. Toss the apples in the kimchi puree. You can do this just before making the salad or up to 6 hours in advance—any longer, though, and the apples will be sublimated by the kimchi.

2 Combine the labne and maple syrup in a small bowl, and whisk together until they're married in a smooth and homogeneous mixture. It should be assertively sweet from the syrup and perceptibly tart from the labne. Adjust if necessary, but don't play down the sweetness too much. You can do this days in advance and keep the labne-syrup mixture in the fridge—it's good with granola or spread thickly on a piece of toast.

3 Heat the oven to 350° (180°C).

4 Arrange the bacon on a rimmed baking sheet, and pop it into the oven. Bake at 350° (180°C) for 18 minutes or until the bacon is browned and crisped. Transfer the meat to a plate lined with paper towels to drain. It needn't be any more than lukewarm when you serve the salad, but it shouldn't be cold or greasy. (If you're preparing all the elements in advance, slightly undercook the bacon up to a couple of hours ahead of time, and then reheat and recrisp it in a 200° (90°C) to 300° (150°C) oven.)

5 Just before serving, toss the arugula with the olive oil, a large dash (0.5 ml) of salt, and a few turns of black pepper.

6 To serve, plop a dollop—1 to 2 tablespoons (15 to 30 ml)—of the sweetened labne in the middle of each plate, and top with one-fourth of the kimchi apples. Stack 3 or 4 pieces of bacon over the apples, and drop a handful of the dressed arugula over the bacon. Hit each plate with a couple of turns of black pepper, and serve at once.

Leah Chase

Dooky Chase's / New Orleans, LA

Leah Chase, destined to become the matriarch of New Orleans Creole cooking, was born in 1923, the oldest of Hortensia and Charles Lange's 11 children, and raised in small town Madisonville, Louisiana. There was no high school nearby for black students, so when she was 13, Chase's parents sent her across Lake Pontchartrain by steamer to New Orleans to live with an aunt and attend St. Mary's Academy. Chase returned home after graduating at age 16, but two years later departed for New Orleans for good. "Creole girls like me were expected to work at the sewing factory, a good job," Chase explained in her oral history. But that was not for her. Eventually she found a job waiting tables for a dollar a day plus tips in the French Quarter. It was a job she credits as "one of the best things that could have happened."

"Unlike many chefs who will say that they cooked with their mothers or grandmothers, not I. I learned the basics at home," said Chase. "My great love for the kitchen came when I started to work in a restaurant as a waitress. The restaurant kitchen was so very different than home. Instead of beans, vegetables, stews, and soups, I saw the preparation of many different sauces and new ways of preparing food. My greatest pleasure was seeing how happy that food made people feel. I began to study and try my hand in the kitchen. I love creating new dishes and adding a little more to those I learned from Mother."

In 1946 Chase married trumpet player and orchestra conductor Edgar "Dooky" Chase II. The couple had four children, and eventually Chase went to work in her in-laws' small sandwich shop. Housed in a double shotgun house, it was a tavern serving po'boys on Orleans Avenue. Chase helped turn the establishment into a full-service affair. Dooky Chase's Restaurant became and remains one of the most important Creole restaurants in the country. Chase, anointed the queen of Creole cuisine, has been in the kitchen ever since, serving fried chicken, stuffed shrimp, chicken Creole, shrimp Clemenceau, and what is widely regarded as the Big Easy's definitive Creole gumbo.

During the 1960s, New Orleans was deeply segregated, and Dooky Chase's was one of the few public places where mixed-race groups could meet to discuss strategy for the local Civil Rights Movement. "Everybody likes a bowl of gumbo," she said. "I like to think we changed the course of America in this restaurant over a bowl of gumbo."

The list of those who have dropped in to dine at Dooky's includes Martin Luther King Jr., James Baldwin, Ray Charles, Thurgood Marshall, George W. Bush, and Barack Obama, whom she playfully chastised for adding hot sauce to her gumbo. Chase was inducted into the James Beard Foundation's Who's Who of Food and Beverage in America in 2010 and has written two cookbooks, *The Dooky Chase Cookbook* and *And Still I Cook*.

Chase has received multiple awards from the NAACP, a Lifetime Achievement Award from the Southern Foodways Alliance, the New Orleans *Times-Picayune's* 1997 Loving Cup Award, the Weiss Award from the New Orleans Council for Community and Justice, and the Outstanding Woman Award from the National Council of Negro Women.

Chef Leah Chase's

SHRIMP CLEMENCEAU

This recipe is a one-dish meal served with a tossed salad, preferably with Italian dressing. Diced chicken breast can be used in place of shrimp. Garnish with a sliced strawberry for a pop of color.

24 shrimp, peeled and deveined

Salt and freshly ground black pepper to taste

½ cup butter (112 g)

4 garlic cloves, finely chopped

4 mushrooms, sliced

½ cup frozen green peas (67 g)

2 cups diced cooked potatoes (450 g)

2 tablespoons chopped fresh parsley (30 mL)

½ teaspoon paprika (2 mL)

1 Season shrimp with salt and pepper. Melt butter in large skillet. Add shrimp and garlic; stir, careful not to burn garlic. Cook until shrimp are pink. Add mushrooms and peas. Cook for about 5 minutes. Add diced potatoes, parsley, and paprika; toss well. Add salt and pepper to taste. Cook until flavors blend well.

Tom Colicchio

Craft / New York

Rare is the self-taught chef who achieves the success and acclaim of Tom Colicchio: chef-founder of two standard-setting New York restaurants, builder of a culinary empire, and compelling TV host.

Colicchio learned to cook from his mother and his grandmother, studied Jacques Pépin's *La Technique* and *La Méthode,* and began working as a teen in a local seafood restaurant in his hometown of Elizabeth, New Jersey, a few miles, but a world away, from Manhattan. A move to New York soon landed the ambitious young cook in the kitchen of the über-trendy Quilted Giraffe, a pioneer of high-end American cooking. He later cooked at Gotham Bar & Grill and at Mondrian, where he was named one of the top 10 best new chefs by *Food & Wine.*

Then, in 1994, Colicchio opened Gramercy Tavern with the great restaurateur Danny Meyer. Gramercy forged a new path for exuberant, confident American cooking, and Colicchio won the James Beard Best Chef: New York award in 2000. A year later, Colicchio left Gramercy to open Craft, which was known for its pithy menu and tightly focused cooking and which celebrated ingredients above all. It won the James Beard Best New Restaurant award in 2002. As Craft led to Craftbar, Craftsteak, and 'wichcraft (a chain of sandwich joints) in New York and nationally, Colicchio's canny business sense became clear. Today, beyond those restaurants, he runs Colicchio & Sons in Manhattan (it earned three stars from the *Times*) and Tom Colicchio's Heritage Steak in Las Vegas, where aged beef is cooked over open fire and coals.

Colicchio is the author of three cookbooks, including *Think Life a Chef* and *Craft of Cooking.*

Chef Tom Colicchio's

CHICKEN SOUP

1 chicken, quartered, with bones intact (do not remove breast meat from breast-bone), including necks and giblets

2 carrots, peeled and halved

2 celery stalks, trimmed and halved

2 leeks, washed and halved

2 parsnips, peeled and halved

1 onion, peeled and halved

1 thyme sprig

Kosher salt

Freshly ground black pepper

1½ cups small shell pasta (150 g) (optional)

Freshly grated Parmigiano-Reggiano cheese (optional)

Extra-virgin olive oil (optional)

Coarse sea salt

This soup is a typical, relaxed Sunday evening meal for my family and me. I serve this soup the way my grandmother did, with the Parmigiano and olive oil. Every grandmother has a chicken soup recipe, so mine certainly isn't the definitive one, but it's still my favorite, and I enjoy sharing that with my kids today the same way my grandmother did with me.

1 Place 1 gallon (3.8 L) water and the chicken in a stockpot, and bring to a simmer over medium heat. Simmer gently, skimming regularly, until broth is fragrant, about 30 minutes. Add the vegetables and thyme, and continue to simmer for another 20 minutes. Season with salt and pepper.

2 For the pasta (if using), bring a large pot of salted water to a boil over high heat. Add the pasta, and cook 8 minutes or until tender; drain. Divide the cooked pasta among 4 bowls.

3 Remove the chicken with a slotted spoon, and place on a serving dish. Ladle the broth and vegetables over the pasta, and serve with grated Parmigiano-Reggiano cheese, more freshly ground black pepper, and a drizzle of extra-virgin olive oil, if desired. Sprinkle the chicken with coarse sea salt, and serve alongside the soup, and serve alongside the soup, or cut into chunks an drop into soup, to serve.

Cat Cora

Kouzzina / Orlando, FL

Cat Cora grew up in an intimate Greek community in Mississippi. Thus did two vigorous food cultures—Southern and Mediterranean—merge in a family home where, she says, "food was the center of life." Meals often combined local spices with cheeses and home-cured olives sent by her Greek relatives. It makes sense that Cora's first cookbook, *Cat Cora's Kitchen,* speaks to that heritage and contains many of her family's favorite dishes.

"Both my families—in Jackson, Mississippi, and on the island Skopelos in Greece—share a love of good food, a passion for gathering around a table for long conversations with family and friends, and a generosity of spirit that reaches from the Aegean Sea to the American South," she writes in the book.

To train as a chef, Cora left Mississippi on the advice of none other than Julia Child. "She was coming close by for a book signing," Cora told AllThingsGirl.com. "I went, and when I got up to her, I asked her the question about becoming a chef. She stopped the signing to talk to me, and she inspired me so much that I enrolled at the Culinary Institute of America the next day."

Cora worked in two New York restaurants before heading to Europe to train with two of France's most esteemed three-star Michelin chefs, Georges Blanc of Vonnas and Roger Vergé. She has since launched several restaurants, including Kouzzina by Cat Cora at Walt Disney World's BoardWalk Inn in Orlando, Florida. Kouzzina serves personal Greek favorites such as *briami* (oven-roasted vegetables, oregano, and Mizithra cheese served with herbed orzo) and *pastitsio,* the classic, cinnamon-tinged Greek version of lasagna. She's also opened three Cat Cora's Kitchens in U.S. airports.

Cora debuted on the Food Network in 1999 on *Melting Pot* and has been a familiar face on foodie television since, most recently on Bravo's *Around the World in 80 Plates.* In 2005, Cora became the first female Iron Chef. She has written three cookbooks and is president and founder of Chefs for Humanity, an organization developed in response to the 2004 Southeast Asia tsunami and modeled after Doctors Without Borders. She is also a nutritional spokesperson for UNICEF.

CHICKEN STEWED IN GARLIC & CINNAMON (KOTA KAPAMA)

My mom always worked, and yet somehow, every birthday, she pulled out all the stops and made exactly what we wanted for dinner. What I wanted, every year, was *kota kapama*. Exceptionally tender and flavorful, *kota kapama* is one of those dishes that sits on the back of the stove all afternoon, filling the house with lush aromas. I liked it so much I'd bribe my younger brother, Chris, to ask for it on his birthday, too.

This dish stews for a long time and is low in saturated fat because it uses olive oil instead of butter or cream. The chicken is flavored with a touch of cinnamon, which is traditional in the Greek diet. I like to serve this with my family's homemade buttered noodles, but it's also great over rice, orzo, or macaroni. The cheese is optional.

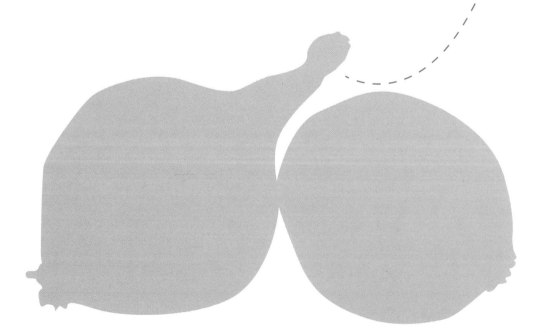

1 (2½- to 3-pound) chicken (1.1 to 1.4 kg), cut into 8 pieces

1 teaspoon ground cinnamon (5 mL)

2 teaspoons kosher salt (10 mL)

1 teaspoon freshly ground black pepper (5 mL)

5 cloves garlic

2 tablespoons extra-virgin olive oil (30 mL)

2 medium yellow onions, peeled and coarsely chopped

½ cup dry white wine (120 mL)

2 cups water (480 mL)

1 (6-ounce) can tomato paste (170 g)

½ cup grated Mizithra cheese (50 g)

1 Pat the chicken dry with paper towels. A wet chicken will cause the oil to splatter while the chicken is sautéing. Combine the cinnamon, salt, and pepper in a small bowl. Rub the chicken pieces on all sides with the seasoning.

2 Mince 3 of the garlic cloves. Heat the olive oil in a large, nonaluminum, deep skillet over high heat. A 12-inch skillet (30 cm) with sides about 2½ to 3 inches high (6.25 cm to 7.5 cm) will allow you to brown all the chicken at once. If you don't have a skillet large enough, brown it in 2 batches using half the oil for each batch. What's important is that the chicken isn't overcrowded, which would cause it to steam rather than brown. Add the chicken to the oil, and brown for about 4 to 5 minutes on each side. Turn the pieces using a metal spatula, as they have a tendency to stick to the pan. Remove the pieces when they are well browned on all sides.

3 Lower the heat to medium-high, and add the onions and minced garlic. Cook for about 3 minutes, stirring constantly, until the onions have softened and are a rich golden brown. Add the wine, and scrape the bottom of the pan with a spatula or spoon to deglaze the pan, loosening any particles stuck on the bottom.

4 When the wine has evaporated, add 2 cups (480 ml) water, tomato paste, and remaining 2 whole garlic cloves. Return the chicken to the pan. The liquid should cover about three-fourths of the chicken pieces. Cover the pot, and simmer over low heat for about 1 hour or until the chicken is tender and thoroughly cooked. If the sauce becomes too thick, it can be thinned with a little more water. Season the finished sauce with kosher salt and pepper to taste. Sprinkle the grated cheese over each serving.

Giada de Laurentiis

Giada at Home | Food Network

Giada de Laurentiis was born in Rome to a family that was best known for its small pasta factory in Naples until her grandfather Dino de Laurentiis, who had sold noodles as a teenager, famously succeeded as a film producer—first in Italy, and later in Hollywood. Giada and her family followed Dino to America, moving from Italy to New York before settling in Los Angeles a year later. Giada was 7. In the early 1980s, Dino reconnected with his family's heritage by opening DDL Foodshow in New York and Los Angeles (a business that the *New York Times* called "a dazzling movie set of a delicatessen.") Giada, too, was dazzled: "I loved the reaction when people walked through that door. They were like little kids in a candy store, and I thought, 'I want to do that someday. I want people to be that excited with my food.'"

After graduating from UCLA with a degree in anthropology, de Laurentiis decided to continue as a student in the kitchen, enrolling at Le Cordon Bleu in Paris. It was in France that she came to understand how deeply passionate a person could be about food. "Now I take classic dishes and reinvent them, and I think a lot of that came from going to school in Paris," she says.

De Laurentiis returned to Los Angeles to work at The Ritz-Carlton and at Wolfgang Puck's Spago. She founded a catering company, GDL Foods. Then television found her. Her 2003 TV debut, *Everyday Italian,* came about after a Food Network executive read an article she'd written for *Food & Wine* about her family's long-ago Sunday gatherings. That Emmy-winning show led to *Giada's Weekend Getaways* and *Giada at Home.* She is the author of seven cookbooks; her most recent, *Giada's Feel Good Food,* was published in 2013.

Finding herself with one hand in food and the other in entertainment, de Laurentiis cites her grandfather's influence as the unifying theme. "I would have to say Nonno Dino was my inspiration in many different ways," she says. "He would have people over for breakfast, lunch, or dinner. In everybody's memory of him, there's always food."

Chef Giada de Laurentiis's

VEGETABLE PARMESAN

It's often been said that to find the best food in Italy you need to be invited to someone's house for a home-cooked meal. It's those simple dishes, lovingly prepared and designed to make good use of what is seasonal, available, affordable—even leftovers—that have always been my favorites and have most strongly influenced the way I cook at home to this day. I think of those dishes as "old world" cooking, and they remain the staples of my repertoire.

The vegetables can also be baked in a 375° (190°C) oven for 15 to 20 minutes, until softened.

Butter for greasing

1 medium eggplant, cut into ¼- to ½-inch-thick slices (6 to 13 mm)

2 medium fennel bulbs, trimmed and sliced into ¼-inch-thick pieces (6 mm)

1 red bell pepper, cut into thirds

1 yellow bell pepper, cut into thirds

1 orange bell pepper, cut into thirds

¼ cup olive oil (60 mL), plus more for drizzling

Kosher salt

Freshly ground black pepper

1 (26-ounce) jar marinara sauce (737 g)

3 cups shredded mozzarella cheese (340 g)

1 cup grated Parmesan cheese (100 g)

1 cup plain breadcrumbs (100 g)

1. Place a grill pan over medium-high heat, or preheat a gas or charcoal grill. Place an oven rack in the center of the oven. Preheat the oven to 375° (190°C). Butter a 13 x 9-inch glass baking dish (33 x 23 cm).

2. Toss the eggplant slices, fennel slices, and peppers with ¼ cup (60 ml) olive oil. Season with salt and pepper. Grill the vegetables for 3 to 4 minutes on each side, until softened.

3. Spoon ¾ cup (180 ml) of the marinara sauce over the bottom of the prepared baking dish. Arrange the eggplant slices on top. Sprinkle with 1 cup (113 g) mozzarella cheese and ⅓ cup (30 g) Parmesan cheese. Arrange the peppers in a single layer on top. Spoon ¾ cup (180 ml) marinara sauce over the peppers. Sprinkle with 1 cup (113 g) mozzarella cheese and ⅓ cup (30 g) Parmesan cheese. Place the fennel on top, and cover with the remaining sauce. Sprinkle the remaining cheeses on top. Sprinkle the breadcrumbs over the cheese, and drizzle liberally with oil. Bake at 375° (190°C) for 30 to 35 minutes, until the top is golden and forms a crust. Cool for 10 minutes before serving.

Bobby Flay

Mesa Grill / Las Vegas

Bobby Flay is a quintessentially American chef: expert interpreter of the vibrant flavors of the American Southwest, as expressed in his first restaurant, Mesa Grill; early champion of Spanish tapas and seafood at Bolo; and pitch-perfect packager of New American cooking with a Southern accent in Bar Americain. He's a born-and-bred New Yorker who displayed an early interest in food, dropped out of high school, was frog-marched by his father into a busboy job, and then charmed and fought his way to the top of his trade.

When he was still a teen, Flay attended the French Culinary Institute in Manhattan, graduating with distinction in 1993, then talked his way into the kitchen of one of the stars of American cooking, Jonathan Waxman, where he fell for the spices and styles of the Southwest. At 26, he opened his Southwest-focused Mesa Grill, quickly winning *New York* Magazine and James Beard Awards.

Flay's cooking is consistently robust, direct, satisfying. His restaurant empire includes Mesa Grills in the Bahamas and Las Vegas; two Bar Americains; a steak joint; and a chain of hamburger restaurants. He rules on TV as well, having several shows—Food Network's *Throwdown!* and *Grill It!* and the Cooking Channel's *Brunch @ Bobby's*—but is perhaps best known as a supremely confident competitor on *Iron Chef America* and a team leader on *Food Network Star.*

Chef Bobby Flay's

FULTON FISH MARKET CIOPPINO

I love cioppino, and I have a lot of experience cooking it, as I serve versions of this flavorful fisherman's soup, which originated in the San Francisco Bay Area, at both Bar Americain and Mesa Grill. My seafood of choice is usually sea bass, shrimp, clams, and oysters but can vary according to what is fresh on any given day. I sneak in anchovies ... not into the broth but in the butter on the croutons served with the soup.

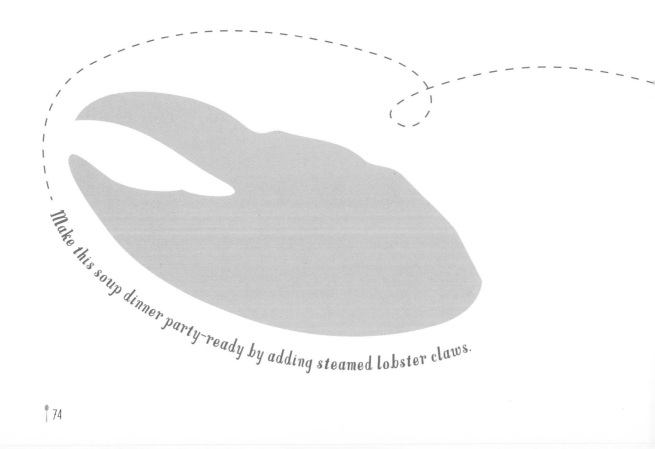

Make this soup dinner party-ready by adding steamed lobster claws.

6 tablespoons olive oil, divided (90 mL)

1 large onion, finely chopped

6 garlic cloves, finely chopped

¼ teaspoon ground red pepper (1 mL)

1 cup dry white wine (240 mL)

5 cups fish stock (1.2 L)

1 (16-ounce) can diced tomatoes, drained (450 g)

1 bay leaf

6 sprigs fresh thyme

Salt

Freshly ground black pepper

1½ pounds bass fillets (720 g), cut into 2-inch squares (5 cm)

12 large shrimp, shelled and deveined

32 littleneck clams

24 mussels, scrubbed and debearded

¼ cup coarsely chopped fresh parsley leaves (15 g), plus whole parsley leaves for garnish

2 tablespoons chopped fresh tarragon leaves (30 mL)

2 tablespoons honey (30 mL)

A few dashes hot sauce

Sourdough Croutons (recipe follows)

1 In a large Dutch oven over medium-high heat, heat 2 tablespoons (30 ml) oil. Add the onion, and cook until soft, about 3 minutes. Add the garlic and red pepper, and cook until fragrant. Add the wine, and cook until reduced by half. Add the fish stock, drained tomatoes, bay leaf, and thyme, and season with salt and pepper. Bring to a boil, and cook until slightly thickened, stirring occasionally, about 15 minutes.

2 While the broth is cooking, heat 2 tablespoons (30 ml) oil over high heat in a large sauté pan. Season the bass on both sides with salt and pepper, and cook 2 minutes on each side or until golden brown on both sides. Remove bass to a plate.

3 To the same pan, add another 2 tablespoons (30 ml) oil, season the shrimp, and sauté 1 minute on each side or until lightly golden brown. Remove to the plate with the bass.

4 Add the clams and mussels to the reduced broth, and cook until the clams and mussels open, discarding any that do not open, about 3 minutes. Add the bass and shrimp, and cook just to heat through, about 1 minute. Stir in the chopped parsley and tarragon, and season with honey, salt, freshly ground black pepper, and hot sauce. Place 1 slice of the Sourdough Crouton in each bowl, ladle some of the mixture on top, and top with another slice of the crouton. Garnish with parsley leaves, if desired.

8 tablespoons unsalted butter (112 g), at room temperature

4 anchovies in oil, patted dry

Kosher salt

Freshly ground black pepper

8 (½-inch-thick) slices sourdough bread (13 mm)

Olive oil

Sourdough Croutons

1 Preheat a grill pan over medium-high heat, or preheat your broiler.

2 Combine the butter and anchovies in a food processor, and process until smooth; season with salt and pepper. Scrape into a bowl.

3 Brush the bread with oil on one side, and season with salt and pepper. Grill, oil side down, on preheated grill pan until lightly golden brown. If broiling, broil, oil side up, on a baking sheet. Turn over, and continue grilling until lightly golden brown on both sides.

4 Remove bread to a platter, and spread some of the butter mixture on the seasoned side.

Marcella & Giuliano Hazan

Cookbook Authors

Victor Hazen, Marcella's husband, standing in back

A very small group of cooks and chefs are venerated for opening American appetites and kitchens to the possibilities of an entire cuisine. Julia Child did that for French cooking. For Italian, it was the late Marcella Hazan.

Marcella's story would be familiar to many immigrants of the 1950s: A newly married woman from a family with deep food traditions—who herself has little in the way of cooking skills—arrives in New York and suddenly confronts the need to prepare meals for her spouse. In this case, the spouse was Victor Hazan, a food lover who, Marcella recalled in her 1997 book, *Marcella Cucina,* had no patience for an indifferently prepared meal. She consulted cookbooks but largely taught herself by experimentation, having discovered that she had vivid, reliable taste memories. Perhaps because of her doctorate in science, she had a methodical nature that lent itself to recipe replication and, a few years later, to cooking instruction, first out of their apartment. She opened a cooking school—the School of Classic Italian Cooking—in 1969 and in short order found her life transformed by Craig Claiborne, the tastemaking food editor of the *New York Times.* Recipe contributions to the *Times* led to cookbook offers, and *The Classic Italian Cook Book* came out in 1973. More books followed, and Marcella won James Beard Awards (including the Lifetime Achievement Award in 2000), among others. She ran cooking schools in both the U.S. and Italy, retiring in the late 1990s with her husband to Florida.

Fealty to true Italian flavors and ingredients marked her approach, along with a love of the handmade dish and the clear, simple recipe. She insisted that preparing food for family is a fundamental necessity of family life. "The story that 'I don't have time to cook,' I never believe it," she told the Associated Press in 2012, when she was 88 and still teaching and sharing—on Facebook. She was active until her death in 2013.

Like Mother, Like Son

Marcella's son, Giuliano, who contributed the recipe here, began working in his mother's cooking school at the age of 17 and spent much of his childhood in Italy (where, by then, Marcella had a cooking school). He was, Marcella wrote in the introduction to his first book, deeply reverent of the authentic: "You will never find Giuliano asking himself what he can do that is different, but rather, what he can do that tastes good."

That first book was 1993's *The Classic Pasta Cookbook*, a bestseller translated into 12 languages. *Every Night Italian,* a collection of recipes taking no more than 45 minutes to prepare, appeared in 2000. It was followed by *How to Cook Italian* and more. In 2012, Giuliano produced his tribute to his mother, *Hazan Family Favorites,* a collection of his mother's best, "rescued from a fifty-six-year-old notebook and taste memories..."

Though he studied theater, Giuliano developed a love of teaching. He has taught cooking on both sides of the Atlantic for years, and in 2007 won the Cooking Teacher of the Year award from the International Association of Culinary Professionals.

Marcella Hazan's

FAMILY MEATBALLS with TOMATOES & PEAS

These tender, delicate, delicious meatballs have been a family favorite for at least three generations and are comfort food at its best. I remember my maternal grandmother, Nonna Mary, making them and serving them with her wonderfully easy, fail-proof oven-baked rice. I remember my mother packing them in a thermos for my lunch at school. And rarely a month goes by in which our family does not enjoy them together at the dinner table. Our two daughters have now learned how to make them as well and, I hope, will pass them on to their families.

These humble meatballs are a perfect example of how the food we prepare for our family and the memories associated with it become an important legacy we pass on to the next generation. The production of a fresh meal for the family is the manifestation of a bond of affection and kinship, an affirmation of identity that constitutes our family's tradition.

These meatballs can be made ahead of time and kept in the refrigerator for one to two days or in the freezer for up to two months. If reheating over the stove, add a couple of tablespoons (about 30 ml) of water to prevent them from drying out.

1 slice plain white bread

2 tablespoons whole milk (30 ml)

½ small yellow onion

1 pound ground chuck (480 g)

1 large egg

¼ cup freshly grated Parmigiano-Reggiano cheese (25 g)

Dash freshly grated nutmeg (0.5 ml)

Salt

Freshly ground black pepper

¼ cup fine, dry breadcrumbs (25 g)

¼ cup vegetable oil (60 ml)

1 cup canned whole peeled tomatoes with their juice (240 g)

1¼ pounds fresh peas in the pod (600 g) or 7 ounces frozen peas (200 g)

1 Cut away the crust from the slice of bread, and put the bread and milk in a small bowl.

2 Peel and finely chop the onion. Mash the bread and milk to a pulp with your fingers, and put the mixture in a large bowl with the ground meat, onion, egg, Parmigiano-Reggiano, and nutmeg. Season with salt and pepper, and thoroughly mix everything together with your hands. Form the mixture into small, compact meatballs, about 1½ inches (4 cm) in diameter. Put the breadcrumbs in a small, shallow bowl; roll each meatball in the breadcrumbs until coated on all sides.

3 Put the oil in a large skillet or sauté pan that will accommodate all the meatballs snugly; place pan over medium-high heat. When the oil is hot, carefully slide in about half of the meatballs using a large spoon. Lightly brown them on all sides; remove from the skillet, and set aside. Repeat with the remaining meatballs.

4 Pour off most of the oil from the pan, leaving just enough to coat the bottom. Return the pan to medium heat, and add the tomatoes, breaking them into small pieces with a wooden spoon. Lightly season the tomatoes with salt, and then return all of the meatballs to the pan. Adjust the heat so that the tomatoes simmer, and cover the pan, with the lid slightly askew. Cook for about 10 minutes, turning the meatballs once after about 5 minutes.

5 If using fresh peas, shell them. Add the fresh peas after the meatballs have cooked for 20 minutes, and continue cooking for 20 more minutes. If using frozen peas, add them after the meatballs have cooked for 30 minutes, and continue cooking for 10 more minutes. If all the liquid in the pan evaporates before the meatballs are ready, begin adding water, ½ cup (120 ml) at a time, until they are done. Serve hot with good crusty bread or rice.

Ingrid Hoffmann

Simply Delicioso / Food Network

Chef and television host Ingrid Hoffmann slides effort-lessly between Spanish and English when addressing her viewers—a mix of Latinos familiar with her cuisine and Anglos intrigued by what she can teach them. She writes cookbooks, such as her bestselling *Simply Delicioso* and *Latin D'lite,* in both languages and broadcasts her cooking show of 11 years on both the Cooking Channel (as *Simply Delicioso*) and Univision (as *Delicioso*). This is more than a smart strategy to increase visibility: Hoffmann knows that the U.S. Hispanic population is rapidly increasing, including a newer generation of home cooks who may not have grown up with *abuela's* cooking. Add to this another market of burgeoning foodies in search of the authen-tic, and Hoffmann's reach seems boundless.

Hoffmann grew up in Colombia and Curaçao, an island off the Venezuelan coast. Because her father was a pilot for Dutch airline KLM, the family moved all over Latin America, and Hoffmann experienced every iteration of Latin cuisine. Her Spanish mother was a Cordon Bleu–trained chef who ran a catering business and restaurant. In 1985, Hoffmann moved to Miami to open a luxury boutique, but she missed the kitchen and in 1993 opened Rocca with her mother (it closed a few years later). A guest appearance on a local Miami TV show caught the attention of Univi-sion executives, and soon Hoffmann was starring in her own cooking show.

"Come, I want to show you this" is Hoffmann's refrain, inviting the viewer in as she peels a ripe mango or dices a jicama. Recipes are fun and bright, like passion fruit mousse or piña colada chicken tacos. Her cook-ware line, available on HSN and at Walmart, features the tools of her cuisine in modern design: cast-iron *comals* with colorful trivets, stackable salsa servers, and a sleek enamel tamale pot. Hoffmann also volun-teers for NYC's Food Education Fund, Miami's Amigos for Kids, and the Believe for Colombia Foundation.

1 (3- to 4-pound) chicken (1.4 to 1.8 kg), cut into 8 pieces

1 medium yellow onion, quartered, plus ½ yellow onion, thinly sliced

1 cup homemade or canned low-sodium chicken broth (240 mL)

1 cup light beer (240 mL) (such as lager)

3 tablespoons Delicioso Adobo (20 g) (recipe follows)

3 tablespoons Worcestershire sauce (45 mL)

1 cup chopped fresh cilantro leaves (16 g)

6 garlic cloves, roughly chopped

2 cups uncooked white rice (370 g)

1 cup fresh or frozen green peas (120 g)

2 medium carrots, finely diced

8 ounces green beans (240 g), trimmed and quartered

1 cup ketchup (240 g)

1 teaspoon salt (5 mL)

3 tablespoons unsalted butter (42 g)

½ red bell pepper, seeded and thinly sliced

½ green bell pepper, seeded and thinly sliced

1 cup pimiento-stuffed olives (230 g)

Chef Ingrid Hoffmann's

ARROZ CON POLLO

Arroz con pollo **is sort of an emblem for all Latin cuisines. Ingredients are recognizable by everyone, and it is so easy to make. You can serve it for an elegant dinner or for a comforting family meal. It is joy on a plate. My Colombian version means comfort to me; it was my favorite dish growing up. My mom would make it once a week, and I could not wait to get home from school and devour it.**

1 Place the chicken, quartered onion, 1 cup (240 ml) chicken broth, beer, Delicioso Adobo, Worcestershire sauce, half of the cilantro, and garlic in a large pot or skillet over high heat. Bring to a boil; reduce heat to medium-low. Cover and simmer until the chicken is cooked through, 30 to 35 minutes. Remove the chicken to a plate, and set aside to cool. Strain the broth mixture in a fine-mesh sieve over a bowl; discard onion pieces.

2 Pour broth mixture into a measuring cup, and add water to make 4 cups (960 ml) of liquid. Return broth mixture to the pot or skillet, and add the rice, peas, carrots, green beans, ketchup, and salt. Stir well, and bring to a boil. Let the liquid evaporate to just below the level of the rice, about 10 minutes, and then reduce the heat to low. Cover and cook until the rice is tender and fully cooked, 25 minutes.

3 Meanwhile, melt the butter in a large skillet over medium heat. Add the peppers and the sliced onion, and cook until they're tender, 8 minutes. Shred the cooked chicken meat, discarding the skin and bones, and add the chicken to the vegetables. Cook until it is heated through, 2 to 3 minutes. Fluff the rice with a fork and add the chicken and vegetables to the rice mixture. Stir in the olives, sprinkle with the remaining cilantro, and serve.

1 tablespoon lemon pepper
seasoning (15 mL)

1 tablespoon garlic powder (15 mL)

1 tablespoon onion powder or flakes (15 mL)

1 tablespoon dried oregano (15 mL)

1 tablespoon parsley flakes (15 mL)

1 tablespoon achiote powder (15 mL)

1½ teaspoons ground cumin (7 mL)

1 tablespoon salt (15 mL)

Delicioso Adobo

1 Combine all ingredients in a small glass jar with an airtight lid, and
shake to blend. Store in a cool, dry place for up to 2 weeks.

Yield: about ½ cup (55 g)

Emeril Lagasse

Emeril's New Orleans / New Orleans, LA

Emeril Lagasse grew up in Fall River, Massachusetts, in a house where there was always a crowd to watch football and devour his mother Hilda's Portuguese food. Crucially, at a time when everyone was in a rush and TV dinners were considered a modern miracle, Lagasse's family "never went there," he says. "We always had the value of the family table and these cultural influences of growing up and what we did. My dad is French Canadian and my mom is Portuguese, so food from those cultures was always a very important part of growing up."

What they also had were fresh ingredients from his uncle's farm. "That was instilled in me as a child, at 7 or 8. I thought it was normal. I thought milking goats and chasing hogs and picking strawberries and vegetables was just what people did," Lagasse told Relish .com upon the publication of his 2010 cookbook, *Farm to Fork: Cooking Local, Cooking Fresh.*

Lagasse was 10 when he landed his first job washing pots at the local Portuguese bakery. It became clear that cooking was his destiny. He played football and baseball in high school and was a gifted drummer, but when it came time for higher learning, he turned down a scholarship to the New England Conservatory of Music for cooking school at Johnson & Wales—a bold call for a working-class American kid.

"Let's face it, nobody in the early '70s—especially a guy—cooked." Lagasse told *Cigar Aficionado* in 2005. "Especially where I came from."

Lagasse traveled to Paris and Lyon, where he learned classic French cuisine. He worked in New York, Boston, and Philadelphia before heading to the kitchen of Commander's Palace, one of New Orleans's grandest shrines of Creole cooking, in 1982—replacing the legendary Paul Prudhomme.

New Orleans became Lagasse's adopted home, and he became one of the city's most famous champions of new-style Creole and Cajun cooking. In 1990, he opened Emeril's, which rapidly gained critical and popular acclaim. Two years later he opened NOLA. The following year, he published his first cookbook, *Emeril's New New Orleans Cooking.*

By the time Lagasse was in his early thirties, he was a national success, but a second career was soon to bloom in television. It's hard to overestimate the importance of Emeril Lagasse to the then-newborn Food Network, which was founded in 1993. *The Essence of Emeril* and, a few years later, *Emeril Live* proved that cooking could stand as a new pillar of American cable entertainment. In all, Lagasse has starred in more than 2,000 television episodes on multiple networks.

In 2002, Lagasse established the Emeril Lagasse Foundation to support children's educational programs that inspire and mentor young people through the culinary arts, school food and nutrition, and life skills programs. To date he has donated more than $5.5 million to children's causes in New Orleans and Las Vegas and on the Gulf Coast. In March 2011, he dedicated the Emeril Lagasse Foundation Culinary Arts Studio, a four-year culinary arts program for high school students with master-apprentice curriculum at New Orleans Center for the Creative Arts. In 2013, Lagasse was named Humanitarian of the Year by the James Beard Foundation.

His business manages 14 restaurants, and he has authored 18 bestselling cookbooks.

2 tablespoons olive oil (30 ml)

1½ cups finely chopped yellow onion (240 g)

1 tablespoon minced garlic (15 ml)

2 pounds Idaho potatoes (960 g), peeled and cut into ½-inch cubes (13 mm)

7 cups chicken stock or canned low-sodium chicken broth (1.7 L)

Salt and freshly ground black pepper to taste

½ teaspoon crushed red pepper (2 ml)

8 ounces kale (240 g), large stems and ribs removed

8 ounces firm (smoked) chorizo or other hot smoked sausage (240 g), diced or crumbled

½ cup chopped fresh cilantro (8 g)

¼ cup chopped fresh parsley (15 g)

2 tablespoons chopped fresh mint (6 g)

Chef Emeril Lagasse's

NEW-STYLE CALDO VERDE

When I think of a recipe that says home, this hearty soup is it. Everyone of Portuguese descent in my hometown has their own way of making it. This is a slightly updated version of my mom's recipe, and the smell of it simmering on the stove really brings me back.

1 Heat the olive oil over medium-high heat in a large soup pot, and add the onions and garlic. Cook until the onions are wilted, 4 minutes. Add the potatoes and chicken stock, cover, and bring to a boil. Season with salt and pepper, and add the crushed red pepper. Reduce the heat to a simmer and cook, uncovered, until the potatoes are tender, 20 minutes. While the potatoes are cooking, thinly slice the kale. Set aside.

2 When the soup is thick and the potatoes have begun to break down, add the sausage, and cook 5 minutes. Stir in the kale, and simmer until the leaves have softened but are still slightly crunchy and the flavors have melded, 15 minutes. Stir in the cilantro, parsley, and mint, and season to taste with salt and pepper. Serve hot with crusty bread.

Mourad Lahlou

Aziza / San Francisco

In the dedication of Mourad Lahlou's cookbook, *Mourad: New Moroccan,* the chef writes, "To my grandpa, Hajj Ben Seddiq, still and always, my loving guide, my voice, my values, the barometer of my soul and the true author of my story."

Lahlou, who grew up in the ancient medina of Marrakesh, came to the U.S. to study economics, not to cook, and certainly not to become a pioneering chef of modern Moroccan food. He credits his rich childhood food experiences for his change of career.

It was his grandfather who ruled the "twenty-room maze of a building" where he, his mom, and his brother lived after his parents split up. It was his grandfather who would win the daily argument about what would be served for the big midday meal, and his grandfather whom he followed on daily, very social rounds through the markets.

Boys were not taught to cook, but Lahlou spent hours watching the women at work in the family kitchen, "the spiritual center of the home."

After arriving in San Francisco at the age of 18 to study, he found the Moroccan food disappointing and began experimenting in his own kitchen, revisiting his memories and trying to re-create family dishes for himself and friends. He felt he was channeling the women he had so devotedly watched: "It's as if they were all cooking in some kind of genetically inherited trance. But fortunately, I shared their genes."

Lahlou earned his master's in economics in 1996 and had his eye on a Ph.D. when his brother, with whom he had been living, convinced him to participate in a joint venture: a new Moroccan restaurant. It would be a six-month gig, Lahlou stipulated, then back to school. Eighteen years later, he's still cooking, having turned "a lifetime of memories into a career."

After opening Kasbah in Marin County to acclaim, Lahlou wanted to push his cooking forward. California was not Marrakesh. Something was lost in culinary translation, but something else could be gained. He could create bicultural food that was both traditional and modern. To that end, he opened Aziza, named for his mother, in San Francisco in 2001. Thirteen years later it's a Bay Area icon, serving the traditional Moroccan dish *bisteeya*—a phyllo-based pigeon pie with almonds and sugar—as a remarkable duck confit phyllo package spiced with *ras el hanout*; combining short ribs with carrot jam, dates, and mustard *soubric* (a sort of bread pudding); and serving multicourse menus that walk a line between modernist and medina.

As he writes in *Mourad,* "My way of cooking and culinary exploration is really a kind of pruning—constantly adjusting and adapting, welcoming new ways and fresh ideas, and always tending my tree with love."

CLASSIC STEAMED COUSCOUS

Couscous is the national dish of Morocco. It symbolizes
the meaning of family and eating together around a table.
You never serve it individually; it's always in a big mound
on a platter. What's really beautiful about it is the process.
The mom or grandmother makes the couscous on Monday
or Tuesday. Then it dries out on Wednesday. The meats and
vegetables are prepared on Thursday, and everything
steams together on Friday morning.

Making couscous is not an art, necessarily, but it's a craft.
You know it by feel. You roll it in your hand until it gets to the
right texture; then you do it over and over again so the grains
are consistent. One granule doesn't taste like anything, but
when you eat them together, it becomes something really
grand. It exemplifies who we are as Moroccans and the
importance of food.

2½ cups chicken stock (600 mL)

2 tablespoons extra-virgin olive oil (30 mL)

⅛ teaspoon saffron threads (0.5 mL)

2 teaspoons kosher salt (10 mL)

1 medium onion, cut into large pieces

2 large carrots, peeled and
cut into large pieces

1 celery rib, cut into large pieces

12 flat-leaf parsley sprigs

3 cups couscous (520 g) (not instant)

1 Combine 2 cups (480 ml) of the chicken stock, the olive oil, saffron, and salt in a medium pot. Bring to a simmer over medium heat for 5 minutes, stirring to dissolve the salt. Remove from the heat, and let sit at room temperature for 30 minutes to infuse with the flavor of the saffron.

2 Fill the bottom of a *couscoussier* half-full with water. Add the onion, carrots, celery, and parsley, and bring to a simmer. Put the couscous in the terra-cotta tray or a very large bowl, pour the infused stock over it (if you like, strain the liquid so you won't have pieces of saffron in your couscous), and let the couscous absorb the liquid, stirring occasionally, for about 15 minutes. Scoop up some of the couscous and rub it with your fingers to separate any lumps, letting it pour back onto the tray. Keep scooping and rubbing in this way until there are no lumps. Repeatedly separating the couscous into individual grains is an important part of the process, so be diligent and unhurried about this.

3 Meanwhile, increase the heat under the *couscoussier* to bring the water to a gentle boil; add more water if needed to maintain the level. Put the couscous in the steamer basket set over a plate, to catch any grains that might come through (put them back in the basket). Run your fingers lightly over the top to make sure the couscous is evenly distributed, and set it over the gently boiling water. If necessary, carefully wrap a large piece of plastic wrap around the rim of the bottom pot to keep the steam from escaping. Once you see steam coming from the top of the couscous, steam for 30 minutes. (Remember, no lid or covering of any kind goes over the couscous, and don't be tempted to stir it.) Carefully remove the plastic wrap, if you used it, and then the steamer basket. When you do this, always pull the basket toward you so you don't get burned by the escaping steam. Spread the couscous in the terra-cotta tray or bowl, and let it sit until cool enough to handle.

4 Meanwhile, add enough water to the bottom of the *couscoussier* to bring its level back to the halfway point. Return to a boil. Clean and dry the steamer basket, discarding any couscous that stuck to it. Run the couscous through your fingers as you did before to separate all the grains. If you come across any lumps that refuse to separate, discard them.

5 When the couscous is at room temperature, you can begin the second steaming. Return the couscous to the steamer basket, add the plastic wrap if needed, and steam for 15 to 30 minutes. The time will depend on how evenly the couscous is steaming. The couscous will take on a sweaty appearance and will feel tender. Spread the couscous out in the tray or bowl as you did before, and let cool. The couscous can be held at room temperature for several hours before the final steaming.

6 Put the remaining ½ cup chicken stock (125 ml) in a spray bottle or in a bowl. If you have let the couscous sit for a few hours and it is no longer warm, add water to the *couscoussier* to return it to the original level, and bring the liquid to a gentle boil. Put the couscous into the steamer and steam it until it is warm. Then transfer to the terra-cotta tray or bowl and run it through your fingers to separate the grains. You now have warm, almost finished couscous that still needs one last round of steaming.

7 Return the couscous to the basket, set it over the bottom pot, and bring the liquid to a gentle boil. Immediately begin to add the remaining stock, spraying the couscous with 15 to 20 sprays from the spray bottle or drizzling about 2 tablespoons (30 ml) of it over the grains. Continue to add the stock in the same way, and stir occasionally for 15 minutes. (By now, the couscous has released most of its starch, and so, for this steaming, and this one only, stirring is not only okay; it's necessary to fluff the couscous.) Pour the couscous into the tray or bowl. It should have doubled in size to about 6 cups (942 g) during the steaming process. (Discard the steaming liquid and vegetables.)

Padma Lakshmi

Top Chef | Bravo

Padma Lakshmi traces the fine-tuning of her palate to a food-focused New York childhood and, at the center of it, a New York apartment kitchen. Lakshmi and her mother moved to New York from Chennai, India, when Lakshmi was a toddler. When her mother went to work, the little girl was fed by her Peruvian baby-sitter, her Filipino neighbors, and later her mother's Caribbean boyfriend. Lakshmi's mother brought new flavors home each day—salted plums from Chinatown, sugarcane from Spanish Harlem. On visits to India, they would hopscotch through great food cities like Singapore and Tokyo, tasting as they went.

Years later, Lakshmi traveled frequently as a super-model and actress, learning the cuisines of Milan, Rome, Cuba, and Sri Lanka. "With food, there's more that unites us than divides us," she told *People* maga-zine. "Take Asian and South American cooking: there's tamarind, cumin, and cilantro in both."

Now, when not axing renowned chefs on televi-sion—she has been the host of *Top Chef* on Bravo for 10 seasons—Lakshmi keeps things simple. She eats a mostly vegetarian diet, accented with the global flavors she grew up with. Lakshmi's latest cookbook, *Tangy Tart Hot & Sweet*, covers it all, from Keralan crab cakes to Mexican enchiladas and Moroccan *bisteeya*. Despite the book's global reach, ingredients are simple and relatively few, and often surprising: a cilantro-carrot salad with *za'atar*, a Middle Eastern spice mix, or lentil soup spiced with dried chiles. The ease and speediness of many recipes was a natural extension of Lakshmi's childhood, when her mother would manage to whip up an impromptu yet exotic meal in her brief windows of free time.

Black mustard seeds and asafetida powder are found easily at Indian grocery markets.

5 large or 8 small unpeeled green sour mangoes, pitted and diced superfine

Salt

1½ teaspoons cayenne pepper (7 mL)

2 tablespoons canola oil (30 mL)

½ teaspoon black mustard seeds (2 mL)

½ teaspoon asafetida powder (2 mL)

½ tablespoon toasted sesame oil (7 mL)

Chef Padma Lakshmi's

GREEN MANGO CURRY

This is one of my favorite recipes from childhood. It's a staple at all South Indian weddings, and it was always the dish I looked forward to most at a wedding. It's very easy to make; mostly it's the dicing of the mangoes that takes time. But it is a labor of love worth doing. When I can't find sour mangoes I just look for really firm, hard unripe ones; while their taste is slightly sweeter, they are just as delicious. The curry will keep in the fridge for a few days.

1 Place the diced mangoes, salt, and cayenne in a bowl. Set aside.

2 Heat the canola oil in a large frying pan over medium heat; add the mustard seeds. When they start crackling and popping, add the asafetida powder. Remove from the heat after a minute or two—you don't want the mustard seeds to burn. Pour this sizzling oil mixture on top of the mangoes. Stir to mix the mangoes well with the oil and spices.

3 Drizzle the toasted sesame oil over the mangoes. The fruit should be crisp and still raw, warmed only slightly by the heat of the oil. Serve at room temperature.

Edward Lee

610 Magnolia / Louisville, KY

Korean-American chef Edward Lee grew up in Brooklyn, trained and worked in New York, and then moved south to Louisville, Kentucky, where for a decade he's been chef-owner of the celebrated restaurant 610 Magnolia.

Lee fell in love with the South because it shares many of the values he learned in his grandmother's Brooklyn kitchen. "She loved doing things in a very slow, methodical way—and doing them right, spending the whole day making a recipe," Lee remembers. "Those are things that just burned into my brain as memory. I don't even remember the dishes so much as the fun noises and the smells coming from the kitchen. The kitchen was always a very sacred place. It was a place of joy, curiosity, and innovation. Everything starts from there."

Visiting and cooking in Louisville in 2002, Lee was impressed by the restaurants, yes, and by the rise of New Southern cooking and the emerging commitment to local farms—but more than any of that he fell for the food and conversation he discovered when invited into Southern homes.

"That's when I think the whole warmth of Southern food, the culture, and the hospitality started to really make waves with me. I didn't just go to someone's house and have dinner. It was a *production*. There were cocktails and snacks, you sat out on a porch and told stories. You waited until the sun went down before going in to eat. The food was incredible. You ended up on the porch with a bourbon at 1 a.m."

Lee's elegant cooking at his flagship restaurant, 610 Magnolia, is a fusion of French, American, and Southern with restrained Asian notes: beef loin and short rib with bok choy, kimchi, mushrooms, and black garlic; diver scallops with Japanese turnips, greens, and pancetta. In 2013, Lee opened Milkwood, a bar and restaurant featuring "comfort food with an Asian pantry," serving dishes like Vietnamese lamb sausage, octopus bacon, crispy-skin duck with apricot hoisin, and miso-smothered chicken with pickled shiitakes and Carolina butter rice.

He's a three-time finalist for the James Beard Award for Best Chef: Southeast and a winner of *Iron Chef America,* and has appeared on *Top Chef Texas.* His first cookbook, *Smoke and Pickles,* published in 2013, is richly larded with South-meets-Far-East fusion recipes and his spicy-vinegary prose.

Chef Edward Lee's

COLLARDS & KIMCHI

This dish harmonizes two very different worlds that have influenced who I am as a chef today. I grew up in a small Brooklyn apartment filled with my grandmother's jars of Korean miso, pickled peppers, and the fermented cabbage kimchi that accompanied every one of our meals. Its pungency perfumed my grandmother's hands, her leathery skin, her wiry hair. To say it was my comfort food is an understatement. Kimchi was a part of my existence. When I moved to Kentucky, I went without it for a while. It seemed out of place in the Southern landscape that I now called home—until I tucked it into a steaming pot of collard greens with its soulful pot liquor that warmed my belly in ways that brought me back to long-forgotten meals alongside my grandmother. The iconic dish of the South felt right at home with the spicy cabbage of my youth. Like they were meant to be together. A culinary yin and yang.

I love these intense flavors from two cultures that are worlds apart, and somehow they work together harmoniously, as if they belong together. The dish goes nicely with roast lamb or fried chicken.

1 tablespoon lard or bacon fat (15 mL)

1 tablespoon unsalted butter (14 g)

1 cup chopped onion (115 g)

1½ cups diced country ham
(about 10 ounces or 280 g)

1½ pounds collard greens (720 g), washed,
stemmed, and coarsely chopped

2½ cups chicken stock (600 mL)

2 teaspoons soy sauce (10 mL)

1½ tablespoons cider vinegar (22 mL)

8 ounces (1¼ cups or 240 g) store-bought
kimchi, chopped

1 Heat the lard and butter in a medium pot over high heat. Once the butter starts to foam, add the onions, and sauté 5 minutes or until they get a little color. Add the ham, and cook 3 minutes, until it is crispy but not too brown. Add the collards, chicken stock, and soy sauce; cover, and cook over medium heat for 30 minutes, stirring occasionally. Taste the collards: They should be tender but still have a little chew to them.

2 Add the vinegar to the greens, and cook for 1 minute. Toss the kimchi into the pot with the greens. Mix together, and serve immediately, juices and all.

When buying premade kimchi from an Asian market, pick one that is well ripened. Look for cabbage that is almost translucent, and notice a smell. Ripe kimchi can smell pungent and sour even through a glass jar.

Sandra Lee

Semi-Homemade Cooking / Food Network

Sandra Lee's improbable story might have been written by Horatio Alger, had he lived to the second Gilded Age. At 11, she was filling in for her ill mother—cooking, cleaning, and taking care of her four younger siblings. By her early twenties she had harnessed her can-do pluck to create a home-decorating kit, Kurtain Kraft, that grossed $6 million in just nine months. QVC quickly hired her as on-air talent, and she sold $20 million worth of products in just 18 months. In her thirties, she penned the first of 26 cookbooks, *Semi-Homemade Cooking,* which landed on the *New York Times*'s bestseller list.

Lee's childhood helped her become not only well versed in all things domestic, but also skilled at relating to those with good intentions, little time, and the need to stretch a dollar. Her recipe approach combines store-bought items with fresh ingredients and found its way to TV when *Semi-Homemade Cooking with Sandra Lee* debuted on the Food Network in 2003. Lee currently hosts three other food-related shows.

After such success, Lee devotes a great deal of her time to the causes of hunger, poverty, and homelessness. She is the national spokesperson for Share Our Strength's No Kid Hungry campaign and the anchor of its largest annual fundraiser, The Great American Bake Sale. She is a founding member of UNICEF's board of directors, Los Angeles chapter, and works with numerous other philanthropic organizations, including The Bowery Mission, God's Love We Deliver, and various food banks. She has received The President's Volunteer Service Award and the Ellis Island Medal of Honor.

12 eggs

¼ cup mayonnaise (55 g)

1 tablespoon Dijon mustard (15 mL)

Zest of 1 lemon

2 teaspoons chopped jalapeños (10 mL)

1 teaspoon smoked paprika (5 mL)

2 tablespoons crumbled bacon for garnish (30 mL)

2 tablespoons chopped fresh chives (30 mL)

Chef Sandra Lee's

ZESTY HOLIDAY DEVILED EGGS

This is one of my favorites because deviled eggs remind me of every joyous occasion, from Easter and summer cookouts to happy holidays with family and friends. They're a breeze to prepare. I make mine with a zesty twist. They always disappear in a snap—everyone in my family between the ages of 4 and 94 loves them. I honestly don't think I could celebrate any momentous event without having them on the table; they're that good.

1 Place eggs in a large pot, and cover with cold water. Bring to a boil, turn off heat, cover, and let sit for 15 minutes. Drain water from pot, and fill with cold water to cool eggs. Change water twice so that the eggs will cool down quickly.

2 Peel eggs, and slice the bottom of each so that it will stand upright. Slice the top third off of each (save tops). Carefully remove eggs yolks with a small spoon, and place them in a medium-size bowl. Break up the egg yolks with a potato masher. Add all remaining ingredients except bacon and chives. Mix until well blended and smooth.

3 Transfer mixture to a resealable bag, cut off the corner of the bag, and pipe filling into each egg. Sprinkle each with chopped chives and bacon bits. Place the tops back onto the eggs. Transfer to a platter, and serve.

Michael Mina

Michael Mina / San Francisco

Egyptian-born chef Michael Mina trained at the Culinary Institute of America in the late 1980s and, a mere four years after his CIA start, found himself devising the launch of a seafood restaurant in San Francisco under the direction of chef and mentor George Morrone, then executive chef of the Bel Air Hotel in Los Angeles. That restaurant, Aqua, opened in 1991 and rapidly became one of the must-try destinations in the Bay Area, serving elegantly plated fish and seafood that earned Mina a Rising Star Chef award from the James Beard Foundation in 1997. By 2002, when Mina left, he had won the Best Chef: Pacific award from Beard.

From there, with partner Andre Agassi, Mina launched the Mina Group, which in its first 11 years opened 17 restaurants. Mina was able to circle back to 252 California St. in San Francisco—where the now-closed Aqua had established his reputation—to open his eponymous restaurant. The restaurant garnered a Michelin star about as quickly as was possible and, in 2011, earned a Restaurant of the Year nod from *Esquire* magazine.

At Michael Mina (there's one in Las Vegas, too), Mina again focuses on seafood, with globally nuanced dishes such as Kona Kampachi sashimi with finger lime, pomegranate gel, shiso oil, and carrot; Morro Bay abalone with Japanese rice, maitake mushroom, pickled beet, and dashi; and duck breast with date, squash, parsnip, and pistachio crumble.

But Mina also runs bars and steakhouses across the country, with widely divergent menus. What ties his food together?

"I love bold-flavored food, and I love balanced food. I like food that keeps me interested throughout the whole course. Don't worry about how to cook everything; start with learning how to taste. What I'm tasting for is balance of acidity, sweetness, spice, and fat. These are the four key ingredients."

He is the author of *Michael Mina: The Cookbook.*

Chef Michael Mina's

FAVA BEAN FALAFEL

Based on my mother's tried-and-true recipe, these falafel are crunchy on the outside and soft and tasty within. A combination of fresh herbs and earthy ground spices gives the falafel their depth of flavor. The fritters get a touch of heat from crushed red pepper, and a pungent kick from garlic and scallions. Falafel is typically made with dried chickpeas, but the seasonal version at Michael Mina uses sweet English peas and earthy fava beans.

2 cups shelled, blanched, and peeled fresh fava beans, or frozen green chickpeas, defrosted (400 g)

½ cup English peas, shelled and blanched, or frozen peas, defrosted (60 g)

¼ cup chopped fresh flat-leaf parsley leaves (15 g)

¼ cup chopped fresh dill (2 g)

¼ cup chopped fresh cilantro (4 g)

3 scallions, green parts only, finely chopped

1 garlic clove, minced

1 teaspoon toasted cumin seeds, ground (5 mL)

1 teaspoon ground coriander (5 mL)

½ teaspoon crushed red pepper (2 mL)

1 teaspoon kosher salt (5 mL)

Freshly ground black pepper

1 cup Wondra flour (125 g)

Grapeseed or canola oil

1 Make sure that favas and peas (or chickpeas and peas) are well drained on paper towels. It is important that the ingredients are dry—this will ensure that the mixture binds properly. Add favas, peas, parsley, dill, cilantro, scallions, and garlic to food processor. Pulse until coarsely chopped. Scrape down the sides of the food processor, and pulse again until the mixture comes together. The mixture should still have some small chunks but be thoroughly mixed. You can tell that it is mixed enough when it comes together in your hand without crumbling. Transfer to a large bowl. Stir in cumin, coriander, crushed red pepper, salt, and freshly ground black pepper.

2 Use a 2-ounce (56 g) scoop (about 2 to 3 tablespoons) to form balls of the chickpea mixture. Press the balls firmly into patties, making sure there are no cracks around the edge. At this point you can fry one patty in 375° (190°C) oil to make sure that the mix is seasoned properly. Hold the patties on a medium-sized baking sheet lined with parchment paper. Chill the patties for at least 1 hour or up to 1 day.

3 Right before frying the falafel, place flour on a baking sheet or baking dish. Gently coat the falafel patties in the flour, dusting off excess. Set a large cast-iron skillet or a large sauté pan over medium-high heat, add ½ to ¾ inch (13 mm to 20 mm) grapeseed or canola oil. Heat oil to 375° (190°C). Add 4 patties at a time to the oil, and cook 2 minutes on each side or until golden brown. Use a slotted spoon or a frying spider to transfer the patties to a plate lined with paper towels. Season with salt. It is important not to overcrowd the pan when frying the falafel. Fry them in batches so that there are at least 2 inches (5 cm) around each one. You can reuse the oil 2 to 3 times. In between batches, scoop out any floating pieces from the oil, and make sure to maintain the oil temperature at 375°. Serve the falafel as a burger with tomato confit and tahini or on their own. A squeeze of fresh lemon juice is the perfect accompaniment.

Marc Murphy

Landmarc / New York

Before he was 12, Marc Murphy had lived in Milan, Paris, Villefranche, Rome, Genoa, and Washington, D.C. Son of an American diplomat, he spent about a decade each in France and Italy, developing a deep love for the food of their classic cuisines. Murphy's French grandmother believed his time was best spent beside her in the kitchen, and she remains one of the biggest culinary influences in his life. His grandfather took him to local shops where samples came freely from behind the counters.

While Murphy chased any European boy's dream of becoming a professional racecar driver, he eventually followed his safer second passion to the Institute of Culinary Education in New York. After graduation, Murphy returned to apprentice in France, armed with language skills and local know-how that would take him deeper into culinary traditions. Chef Alain Ducasse, who saw him at work in his famed Louis XV kitchen in Monte Carlo, gave Murphy the chance to focus his potential under chef Sylvain Portay at the legendary Le Cirque in New York. The restaurant became the launchpad for Murphy's career.

After Le Cirque, Murphy was a New York champion of what Portay taught: "coaxing out the most vibrant, interesting flavors any ingredient had to offer, yet [insisting] on minimal manipulation." He opened Landmarc in 2004, offering bistro classics such as steak with shallot Bordelaise sauce; boudin noir; crispy sweetbreads; and steak tartare. The restaurant's relaxed confidence was a hit in Tribeca. Ditch Plains followed in 2006, featuring casual American dishes like lobster rolls, fried oyster hoagies, seafood Cobb salad, and burgers with smoked slaw and smoked aioli. Next came a bustling branch of Landmarc at the Time Warner Center in 2007.

Murphy is a regular judge on Food Network's *Chopped* and has appeared on *Unique Eats* and *The Best Thing I Ever Ate*. In addition to his restaurant and television responsibilities, he is active in the community. He and his wife, Pamela, serve on City Harvest's Food Council and Share Our Strength's No Kid Hungry task force. As he told Share Our Strength, "As a chef, I can't believe that there are so many children out there who are hungry. My job is to feed people, and I take that literally."

Chef Marc Murphy's

CHESTNUT JAM

This is an old family recipe passed down from my great French aunt. I chose it because it reminds me of my childhood growing up in France and Italy. It was during those years that I developed not only a passion for eating, but a palate for great cuisine and classic, simple ingredients.

2 (14.8-ounce) jars whole roasted chestnuts (420 g)

2 cups granulated sugar (400 g)

2 teaspoons pectin (10 mL)

1 whole vanilla bean

1 cup water (240 mL)

1 Place chestnuts in a medium saucepan, and cover with cold water. Bring to a boil; remove from heat, and drain. Working in batches, press chestnuts through a potato ricer over a bowl. You should have 5 cups (1.2 L) total. Set aside.

2 Place sugar and pectin in a medium saucepan. Halve vanilla bean lengthwise; scrape seeds into sugar mixture, and add bean to pan. Whisk in 1 cup (240 ml) water, and place over low heat, constantly stirring, making sure the sugar dissolves, about 10 minutes. Remove the vanilla bean, and reserve for another use. Add chestnuts, 1 cup (240 ml) at a time, to the sugar mixture, stirring until smooth. Bring mixture to a boil; remove from heat, and let cool. Place jam in an airtight container, and place in the refrigerator. The jam will last up to 2 weeks.

Jamie Oliver

Fifteen / London

Few if any chefs have accomplished as much before the age of 40 as the indefatigable Jamie Oliver, who has had remarkable influence on the restaurant world, the cookbook industry, television, social media, and food-related social causes—while becoming a full-blown mainstream celebrity.

Oliver grew up in Essex, England, where his parents, Trevor and Sally, ran (and still run) The Cricketers in Clavering, a pub/restaurant that was an early entry in the movement to elevate pub fare. Oliver frequently helped in the kitchen and at age 16 left school for training at Westminster Catering College. He worked in France and London, eventually landing at London's famed River Café, where in less than four years he attracted the interest of television producers—and the Oliver rocket was launched.

Many chefs have charity causes, of course, but almost from the start Oliver has leveraged his enormous TV charisma to force a national debate in the U.K. about the quality of school lunches, food-related education, and, more broadly, the place of proper food in the welfare of a nation. Oliver carried the cause to the U.S. with his controversial, two-season, Emmy-winning ABC series *Jamie Oliver's Food Revolution*. In 2002, he created Fifteen, which provides restaurant apprenticeships for 15 disadvantaged young adults a year.

His trajectory has been amazing—leading to a booming chain of Italian restaurants; numerous books and TV shows (with global sales almost too high to believe); extensive involvement in food festivals; and a recent restaurant partnership with grilling guru Adam Perry Lang. It all proceeds from an unstoppable enthusiasm for real food. A consistent and unmistakable voice across all media (he had 1.5 million Instagram followers by the end of 2013), Oliver is boyishly passionate about the pure pleasures of markets, restaurants, gardens, kitchens, and the family table.

Chef Jamie Oliver's

LEIGH-ON-SEA SOLE

This is a great dish I made near my family's historical stomping ground on the Essex coast: Leigh-on-Sea. I used Dover sole, but any sustainable or Marine Stewardship Council–approved flatfish like flounder or lemon sole would also be fantastic. Dover sole can be a bit on the pricey side, but they are so tasty that they are a wonderful treat every now and then. You want them skinned, with the heads left on, so either ask your fishmonger to do this for you or watch the video at jamieoliver.com/videos/how-to-prepare-dover-sole. I've used fresh cockles and peeled salad-size shrimp, which are deliciously sweet but way underrated. This dish is best made for two, so you can cook everything together quickly in one large pan. There's something about the way these ingredients work together that makes it such a luxurious dinner. Hope you love it.

OK, here's a quick pep talk for you: Every house needs an extra-large nonstick frying pan, so if you don't have one, go and get one; otherwise you won't be able to cook two fish at the same time. You will also need a large fish spatula. Cooking flatfish like this is very simple, but you mustn't overcook it. How do you know when it's cooked perfectly? Simple: Gently try to pull the meat away from the thickest part next to the head. If it moves, it's cooked. If it doesn't, it's not.

4½ ounces fresh cockles or small clams (or mussels) (128 g)

2 slices of quality bacon

Olive oil

2 sprigs of fresh rosemary

A small knob of butter

2 Dover sole, skinned (about 1 pound or 480 g)

2 ounces peeled salad-size shrimp (57 g)

A small bunch of fresh chives

2 lemons

Sea salt

Freshly ground black pepper

1 Sort through the cockles or clams, and tap them. If any stay open, throw them away. Give them a wash and slush about in a bowl of cold water. Put a large frying pan on medium heat; slice the bacon into matchsticks. Add the bacon to the pan along with a drizzle of olive oil, and fry until lightly golden. Strip the leaves from the sprigs of rosemary, and add to the pan. Fry for a few more minutes; then remove everything to a plate with a slotted spoon.

2 Add a small knob of butter to the bacon fat, give it a little shake, and carefully lay both fish in the hot pan, head to tail. You're going to cook them at medium-high heat, so it won't take long, but the cooking shouldn't run away from you. Cook the fish for about 4 minutes; then carefully and confidently turn each one over with a large fish spatula. Quickly return the rosemary and bacon to the pan, and add the shrimp and cockles or clams. Using a tea towel to protect your hands, cover the pan immediately with a lid or foil, making it as airtight as you can. Cook for another 4 minutes, or until the cockles have all opened.

3 Finely slice the chives; remove the foil from the pan when the time is up. Squeeze in the juice of a lemon, scatter over the chives, and add a good dash of salt and pepper. Shake the pan around with a sense of urgency, and remove the fish to a warm platter or 2 plates, pouring over all the juices and seafood from the pan. This is nice served with lemon wedges on the side and a simple pea and spinach salad, some buttered asparagus, or new potatoes.

Vitaly Paley

Paley's Place / Portland, OR

Vitaly Paley's first discipline was piano. He started playing at age 6 and studied at Juilliard. But when he describes leaving Russia for Rome in 1976 at age 13 and living in the great Italian city before immigrating to the U.S., what he talks about is the food. "The food there made my head spin," he writes in *The Paley's Place Cookbook: Recipes and Stories from the Pacific Northwest.* "I tasted my very first bite of pizza. My first gelato. The smell of coffee would reel me into a café from a block away. My mother got creative with what little means we had and made sure we ate well, in a way that would pay huge dividends in my adult life ... As the foods around me evolved, my palate evolved with them."

Two years into his studies as a concert pianist, Paley decided to hop from the frying pan of Juilliard into the fire of the French Culinary Institute in New York. His kitchen career began at Union Square Café, Remi, and Chanterelle, all Manhattan stalwarts. Then he moved on to France, where he apprenticed at Moulin de la Gorce near Limoges. In 1994, he and his wife, Kimberly, headed to Portland, Oregon, where they opened Paley's Place. Emphasis has always been on local ingredients in dishes that reflect Paley's diverse background. A recent spring menu offered Kampachi sashimi with quail egg, micro shiso, and lemon ponzu; duck bologna; and seared halibut and spot prawns with a fennel and saffron puree.

In 2005, Paley brought home the James Beard Award for Best Chef: Northwest, and in 2008 published his cookbook. His résumé also includes a 2011 victory on *Iron Chef America.* The next year he opened Imperial, devoted to grilling, as well as Portland Penny Diner.

Russia, Rome, New York, Paris, and Portland— Paley brings all of these influences to the stove, but it began in a one-bedroom house in Russia where his grandmother did the cooking, making cheese and buttermilk and baking bread in a little brick oven and where everything was fresh. "You get to invent with all of your abilities and all of your experiences," he told *About Face* magazine in 2012. "And then you just give it that free Portland spirit, and before you know it, you've got a cuisine of its own."

Chef Vitaly Paley's

POTATO MUSHROOM CAKE

I remember how I used to accompany my grandfather to a farm each fall. We gathered enough potatoes to last through the winter. In our basement my grandfather constructed a clever maze of compartments that would keep the tubers cold and dark. Among the many potato dishes that my grandmother prepared, one in particular stands out in my memory. It was simply tiny pancakes made from raw potatoes grated, mixed with eggs, and fried in duck fat.

I stood by the stove whenever she prepared them, and like a hungry puppy panting for food, I scored the first few pancakes as they came out of the fat. Cooled slightly by sour cream, they burned my fingers as I ate them. Once I had my fill, the more patient members of our clan had their turn.

If I don't have duck fat available, I substitute olive oil.

6 tablespoons of duck fat (75 g), plus more if making individual cakes

1 large porcini mushroom, cleaned, or a king oyster mushroom, coarsely chopped

Salt

Freshly ground black pepper

1 pound Dutch Yellow or Yukon Gold potatoes (480 g), peeled and cut into ¼-inch dice (6 mm)

1 large shallot, peeled and coarsely chopped

2 garlic cloves, finely minced

1 large egg, lightly beaten

3 tablespoons chopped fresh parsley, divided (9 g)

1 Preheat oven to 400° (200°C).

2 In a large skillet, heat 2 tablespoons (30 ml) duck fat over medium heat. Add the mushrooms, season with salt and pepper, and sauté until soft and lightly colored. Drain on paper towels, and set aside to cool.

3 Place the cooked mushrooms, potatoes, shallot, garlic, egg, and 2 tablespoons (30 ml) parsley in the bowl of a food processor. Season liberally with salt and pepper. Pulse about 8 to 10 times, until the mixture is pureed.

4 In a 10-inch (25 cm) nonstick skillet over low to medium heat, melt the remaining duck fat. Pour in the potato mixture, and spread it evenly to the edges using a rubber spatula. Cook the cake, undisturbed, until the edges turn light brown, about 5 minutes. Place a large, shallow platter or a large, flat pot cover over the pan; then invert the cake onto it. Gently slide the cake back into the skillet, and place it in the oven. Bake at 400° (200°C) until potatoes are completely done and cake is springy to the touch, about 30 minutes. Slide the cake onto the serving platter, and slice it into 12 wedges.

5 To make individual potato cakes, melt duck fat in a medium skillet over medium heat. Spoon small dollops of potato batter into the pan, and brown 2 to 3 minutes on each side. Repeat with remaining batter. Serve hot or at room temperature. Sprinkle pancakes with remaining parsley, and serve.

Cindy Pawlcyn

Mustards Grill / Napa Valley, CA

"I often ask my family what *country* they want dinner from," says Cindy Pawlcyn. The California chef has spent three decades creating farm-to-table cuisine at her Napa Valley restaurants—Mustards Grill, Cindy's Backstreet Kitchen, and Cindy Pawlcyn's Wood Grill & Wine Bar (CP's). But as local as her sourcing is, the inspirations have been decidedly global.

Her childhood family was inclined that way: Pawlcyn grew up eating tomatoes from their Minnesota family garden and fishing for dinners with her dad and uncle, but she was out with her mom every Monday for Thai, Vietnamese, Chinese, French—just about anything other than the Russian/Austrian/German/Norwegian fare her parents had grown up with.

At 13, Pawlcyn began working at a local cooking school. "I took the Indian cooking class and the Chinese cooking class, and I'd come home and cook," she says. "My dad would eat anything as long as we made it ourselves and it wasn't store-bought."

After college, Pawlcyn trained at Le Cordon Bleu and La Varenne in Paris. Her early restaurant work was in the Midwest before she headed to San Francisco in 1979. The California food revolution was underway, and she landed a gig as the first chef at Napa Valley's luxury Meadowood Resort.

Pawlcyn was instrumental in founding two restaurants that became icons of California cuisine: Mustards Grill in Napa in 1983 (eclectic farm-to-table wine country fare) and Fog City Diner in 1985 (globally inflected small plates in a good-time, polished retro diner setting). She has been involved in the opening of more than a dozen Bay Area restaurants. Today, her menus are all about the happy jostle of influences: Oysters Bingo bumps up on the menu with ahi tuna with buckwheat noodles and wasabi vinaigrette; Famous Mongolian Pork Chops are next to sweet corn tamales.

Along the way, Pawlcyn has written five cookbooks, including the James Beard Award–winning *Mustards Grill Napa Valley Cookbook,* the *Fog City Diner Cookbook,* and, most recently, *Cindy's Supper Club: Meals From Around the World to Share With Family and Friends.*

She likes the similarities that pop up in vastly different culinary cultures: "The Georgian chicken recipe I've selected for this book has an awful lot of garlic and black pepper. There's another recipe, a Thai dish, that you cook and prepare differently, but it's the same thing—mostly garlic and black pepper."

Chef Cindy Pawlcyn's

CLASSIC GEORGIAN "PRESSED" CHICKEN with WALNUT & BEET SAUCES

This recipe reminds me of the way my dad put food together. He came over here in 1918 when he was a teenager, and all of his life he had had that old country cooking. He'd pan-fry it the way his mom did. When I have it, I feel like I am eating my ancestral heritage, and I think it's funny that when I eat that kind of food it really hits the spot. I guess somewhere in the DNA of this dish is home.

I make this with *poussins*, but it could easily be made with chicken thighs or breasts, boneless half chickens, or Cornish hens. If you use *poussins* or Cornish hens, you will need one bird per person. The parchment paper keeps the skin of the birds from sticking to the pan you are using as a weight. If you don't have a pan to use as a weight, use a couple of bricks wrapped in aluminum foil. You can also skip the pressing step, though the dish won't be authentic. If you opt not to press, make sure the skin still gets very crispy.

The pan juices are finished with a little water or stock and parsley. You can use the backbones and wing tips that you removed from the birds to make a quick stock to use for the liquid. The walnut sauce and the beet sauce are delicious with these birds, but it is fine to make just one of them. Both of them may be made a day ahead and refrigerated, saving you time on serving day. If you only have sweet paprika on the shelf, add a touch of cayenne pepper along with the paprika. The sauce needs a little heat to counter the richness of the nuts. I love the beet sauce on grilled fish as well.

6 poussins

6 tablespoons unsalted butter (84 g)

Sea salt and freshly ground black pepper

2 to 3 garlic cloves, mashed in a mortar

1 cup water or chicken stock (240 mL)

1 cup fresh flat-leaf parsley leaves (60 g), rinsed, minced, and squeezed dry

3 tomatoes, cut into wedges and lightly salted

Walnut Sauce (recipe follows)

Beet Sauce (recipe follows)

1 To prepare the poussins, remove the backbones and wing tips from each bird, or ask your butcher to do it for you. Turn each bird breast side up and, using both hands, press firmly on the breast to break the breastbone and flatten the bird. Place a very large sauté pan (big enough to hold all of the birds with a little space left over) or 2 sauté pans over medium-low heat, and add the butter (dividing it if using 2 pans). While the butter melts, season the birds on both sides with salt and pepper. When the butter is nice and foamy, place the birds, bone side down, in the pan. Cover just the birds, not the pan, with parchment paper, and place a second pan on top of the parchment. Fill the top pan with water (or a weight) to press the birds down, and then "fry" the birds slowly for 25 minutes. Remove the top pan, being careful not to slosh any water into the cooking pan; flip the birds over, skin side down; and replace the parchment, the top pan, and the weight. Cook for another 15 to 20 minutes to crisp the skin and finish cooking the meat.

2 If you don't want to be bothered with pressing the birds on both sides, you can add the birds, bone side down, to the melted butter and cook for about 10 minutes until seared. Then flip the birds skin side down, cover with parchment paper, top with a weighted pan, and cook for 10 to 15 minutes, until done (no additional turning needed).

3 When the birds are ready, pull them out of the pan, put them on a large platter, and keep them warm. Add 2 to 3 garlic cloves and 1 cup (240 ml) water to the pan juices (dividing them if using 2 pans); increase the heat to high, and cook, stirring to scrape up any browned bits on the pan bottom, until reduced by two-thirds. Stir in the parsley, and remove from the heat. Spoon the pan sauce over the birds, and place the tomato wedges here and there around the platter. Serve the walnut and beet sauces on the side.

1 cup walnuts (110 g)

1 to 2 garlic cloves

1½ to 2 teaspoons ground coriander (7 to 10 mL)

1 teaspoon hot paprika (5 mL)

2 to 3 teaspoons cider vinegar (10 to 15 mL)

Up to 1 cup water, as needed (240 mL)

Sea salt

Walnut Sauce

1 To make the walnut sauce, combine the walnuts, 1 to 2 garlic cloves, 1½ teaspoons (7 ml) coriander, paprika, and 2 teaspoons (10 ml) vinegar in a blender. With the motor running, slowly add the water, stopping when the sauce is the consistency of thick cream. It should be thinner than mayonnaise but thicker than a rich broth. Taste and season with the remaining vinegar and coriander, if needed, and with salt. Set aside.

2 beets, boiled or roasted, peeled, and finely grated

1 small garlic clove, minced

1 tablespoon olive or walnut oil (15 mL)

2 tablespoons cider or rice vinegar (30 mL)

¾ cup sour cream (170 g) or 6 tablespoons each plain Greek-style yogurt and crème fraîche (85 g)

Sea salt

1 to 2 tablespoons minced fresh cilantro (15 to 30 mL)

Beet Sauce

1 To make the beet sauce, combine the ingredients in a bowl, stirring to combine. Cover and chill before serving.

Wolfgang Puck

Spago / Beverly Hills, CA

Wolfgang Puck is one of a very small and exclusive group of chefs known internationally for innovative cooking, a mastery of restaurant hospitality and the fine art of publicity, an instinct for bold business moves, and a remarkable talent for reinvention.

Puck, who is Austrian, remembers cooking at his mother's side when she was a chef in a small town. Like many Europeans bound for the kitchen, he began the hard work of apprenticing at age 14. As a young chef he worked in top French restaurants: Maxim's in Paris; a Michelin three-star restaurant in Provence; and Hôtel de Paris in Monaco. Then, at 24, he moved to America, working at La Tour in Indianapolis from 1973 to 1975.

It was then that he moved to L.A. and made his mark, first at Ma Maison, then, in 1982, at Spago, which became a local celebrity magnet that generated international buzz. At Spago, California cuisine took a star turn; pizza became haute. Yet Spago was more California-exuberant than Euro-starchy.

Puck was only beginning, and he was in a hurry: Chinois on Main, opened in Santa Monica in 1983, was a trendsetting Asian-French-American fusion restaurant, a decade or more ahead of its time.

Since then, Puck has moved Spago and reinvented it to acclaim (the latest menu offers dishes like veal filet mignon tartare with smoked mascarpone); diversified into manufactured foods and airport outlets; starred on TV; catered the famous Governor's Ball after the Academy Awards; and opened more than 100 restaurants around the world. Puck is the only chef to win the James Beard Outstanding Chef of the Year award twice, and he won the Beard Lifetime Achievement Award in 2012. His trademark tireless congeniality, combined with precision and inventive cooking, set the standard for chefs in the U.S.

½ pound whole shelled hazelnuts (240 g)

1 cup cake flour, plus more for dusting (137 g)

½ cup all-purpose flour, plus more for dusting (63 g)

½ pound unsalted butter (240 g), at room temperature if using a hand mixer

1 cup sugar (200 g)

1 egg

½ teaspoon ground cinnamon (2 ml)

¼ teaspoon freshly grated nutmeg (1 ml)

¼ teaspoon ground cloves (1 ml)

¼ teaspoon salt (1 ml)

1 teaspoon grated lemon zest (5 ml)

1 cup raspberry jam (320 g)

Powdered sugar for dusting

Chef Wolfgang Puck's

MOTHER'S LINZER COOKIES

My mother would always begin baking in early December and keep it up right through the holidays. The smell of cinnamon, nutmeg, and cloves baking in the oven reminds me of my childhood growing up in Austria, and this recipe is one of my favorites.

1 Preheat oven to 350° (180°C).

2 Spread the hazelnuts in a single layer on a baking sheet, and toast them at 350° (180°C) until golden, 10 to 12 minutes. Empty them into a folded kitchen towel, enclosing them between the folds, and rub them to remove their skins. Discard skins. Transfer the nuts to a food processor fitted with the stainless-steel blade. Add the flours. Process until the nuts are finely ground.

3 In a stand mixer fitted with the paddle attachment, or in a large mixing bowl with a handheld electric mixer, beat the butter and sugar together at medium-high speed until light and fluffy. Add the egg, cinnamon, nutmeg, cloves, salt, and lemon zest, and continue mixing for 1 minute. Reduce the speed to low, and gradually add the nut-flour mixture. Mix just until the mixture comes together into a smooth dough. Scrape the dough onto a sheet of plastic wrap, and gently press it into a flat disc, about 2 inches (5 cm) thick. Wrap the dough in plastic wrap, and refrigerate for at least 2 to 3 hours, or preferably overnight.

4 Remove the dough from the refrigerator, and divide it into quarters. Place 1 piece between two sheets of lightly dusted parchment paper, and roll out to an even ⅛-inch (3 mm) thickness. Repeat with the other pieces of dough. Place dough in the freezer 15 minutes or until chilled.

5 Preheat the oven to 350° (180°C).

6 Place the oven rack in the lower third of the oven. Line baking sheets with parchment paper. Remove the dough from the freezer, 1 sheet at a time. Carefully peel the top piece of parchment off the dough, and, using a round 2-inch (5 cm) fluted or straight-edged cookie cutter, cut out circles of dough. With a ½-inch-diameter (13 mm) circular cookie cutter, cut out holes from the centers of half of the larger circles, giving them shapes resembling rings (the holes will make nice mini cookies).

7 Carefully transfer the cookies to the baking sheets, about ½ inch (13 mm) apart. If the dough is too soft to transfer easily, return it to the freezer for 15 to 30 minutes. If you need to bake the cookies in batches, make sure you let the baking sheets cool before baking each batch. Bake the cookies at 350° (180°C) until golden brown, 10 to 14 minutes. Slide the parchment onto cooling racks, and wait 10 minutes; then carefully transfer the cookies to the racks to cool completely.

8 Return the cookies to your work surface. Place a scant teaspoon (5 ml) of jam on each cookie without the holes, and spread in an even layer. Generously dust the cookies with the holes with powdered sugar, either from a sugar sifter or from a fine-mesh sieve held over the cookies and tapped with your hand, and neatly place them on top of the jam so that the jam pokes out the center.

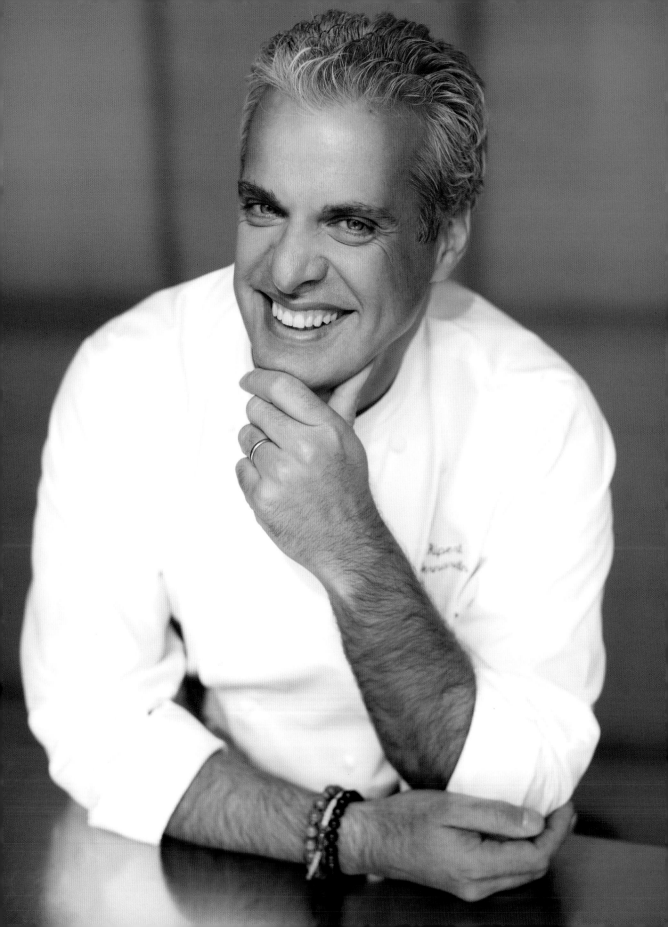

Eric Ripert

Le Bernardin / New York

Eric Ripert reached the pinnacle of the New York chef scene by deploying impeccable skills with one food—seafood—in the kitchen of one restaurant: Le Bernardin. He seems, among his fellow restaurant and food-media stars, one of the most self-possessed, the most focused, and the most *French,* despite having been in the U.S. since 1989.

Ripert grew up in Antibes, France, and in Andorra, a small country between Spain and France, attending culinary school—as many boys did in Europe—at the age of 15. At 17, he was working in Paris at the grand, Michelin-starred La Tour d'Argent and later at Joël Robuchon's Jamin as the chef in charge of fish cookery, setting the course for his future specialty. Moving to the U.S., Ripert had a brief stint in Washington, D.C., and then moved to New York in 1991.

In 1994, Ripert, only 28 years old, became executive chef of Le Bernardin after his predecessor died suddenly of a heart attack. Within a year, the restaurant received a four-star review from the *New York Times,* a rating it has maintained over two decades. Accolades for Le Bernardin have been impressive—multiple Michelin stars, James Beard Awards, and even recognition by *GQ* in 2007 as one of the Seven Food Temples of the World.

Most impressive is Ripert's consistent focus on the purity of ingredients and sharp refinement of technique—French, but tinged with global flavors—as he strives to reveal the essential quality of fish. Ripert's lightness of hand is legendary. The menu divides courses into "almost raw," "barely touched," and "lightly cooked," offering dishes such as ultra-rare smoked sea trout with braised baby leeks and *sauce gribiche;* barely cooked scallop with brown-butter dashi; and poached halibut with opal basil, shaved fennel, and red miso–citrus sauce. The restaurant underwent a complete remodel in 2011, and the menu changes frequently, depending on the best sustainable seafood available.

Ripert often takes his signature style and accent to the small screen, playing a suave counterpart to his rambunctious friend Anthony Bourdain. On *Avec Eric,* he travels the world eating, and then re-creates what he has discovered in his own kitchen. A follow-up series called *On the Table* brings celebrities such as Drew Barrymore and Stanley Tucci into Ripert's kitchen to talk and cook. Ripert also chairs New York's City Harvest Food Council, working with chefs and restaurateurs to increase the quality and quantity of food donations all over the city.

¼ cup extra-virgin olive oil (60 mL)

1 large onion, cut into ½-inch dice (13 mm)

1 red bell pepper, seeded and cut into ½-inch dice (13 mm)

1 banana pepper, seeded and cut into ½-inch dice (13 mm)

4 garlic cloves, thinly sliced

1 tablespoon tomato paste (15 mL)

3 tomatoes, seeded and cut into ½-inch dice (13 mm)

2 small zucchini, cut into ½-inch dice (13 mm)

1 medium eggplant, peeled and cut into ½-inch dice (13 mm)

Fine sea salt

Freshly ground black pepper

4 (6-inch) cocotte dishes (15 cm)

8 eggs

¼ cup grated Parmesan cheese (25 g)

¼ cup julienned fresh basil (12 g)

Chef Eric Ripert's

BAKED EGGS with RATATOUILLE

A favorite French recipe, this dish includes a variation of summer vegetables, including peppers, onions, tomatoes, zucchini, and eggplant, with herbs that are typically grown in Provence, like basil and oregano. With the addition of eggs, it makes for a great, comforting meal.

1 Heat olive oil in a Dutch oven over medium-high heat. Add the onion, red pepper, banana pepper, and garlic, and sauté until tender, about 5 to 7 minutes. Add the tomato paste, and continue cooking for 3 to 5 minutes. Add the tomatoes, zucchini, and eggplant, and cook until tender, about 10 minutes, adding water as necessary. Season to taste with salt and pepper. This can be done up to 2 days ahead and kept refrigerated.

2 Preheat broiler.

3 If the ratatouille was done ahead and kept cold, gently rewarm over medium heat. Spoon about ½ cup (120 mL) of the ratatouille into each cocotte, crack 2 eggs on top of each serving, place the cocottes under the broiler, and cook until the egg whites are just barely set, about 5 minutes; serve hot with Parmesan and basil on top.

Marcus Samuelsson

Red Rooster / New York

New York's Marcus Samuelsson is one of America's most accomplished "chefs, who has mastered, with style and ease, cooking that manages…" to be both local and global.

Samuelsson was born in Ethiopia in 1971. In 1972, his mother died from tuberculosis. Marcus and sister Linda were then adopted by Ann Marie and Lennart Samuelsson of Goteborg, Sweden. Suddenly in Sweden, only 2 years old, he was part of a happy family of food lovers. "Fresh" and "local" were daily facts of eating, and Samuelsson has been cooking as far back as he can remember.

"My sisters Anna and Linda and I spent summers in Smögen, on the west coast of Sweden. Every morning I went fishing with my dad, Lennart, and my uncles. We caught crayfish, lobsters, and mackerel and often smoked and preserved the catch. My grandmother Helga would gather us in the kitchen to teach us how to pickle fresh vegetables and make meatballs, ginger snaps and cookies, and apple jam."

Samuelsson studied cooking in Sweden, apprenticed in Switzerland, and in 1994 landed a job in Manhattan at the innovative Scandinavian restaurant Aquavit, where he rapidly rose to executive chef and earned the restaurant three stars from the *New York Times*. In 2010, he moved uptown to open the convivial, neighborhood-focused Red Rooster, committed to local hiring and the celebration of Harlem culture. On the Red Rooster menu: fried "yardbird" and mashed potatoes, along with ramen made with teff (an Ethiopian grain) and the comfort food of grandma's kitchen, Helga's meatballs.

"Red Rooster fulfills my dream to showcase American comfort food with hints of my Swedish and African roots," the chef says of his local/global vibe. "I want this to be a place where people from all walks of life can break bread together."

Though known for his Swedish and American chops, Samuelsson is deeply influenced by his other window into food: Africa. He returned to Ethiopia for the first time in nearly 30 years in 2000, visiting his biological father and meeting 18 brothers and sisters for the first time. There he witnessed the sharing that binds people in their struggle to survive.

"In Ethiopia, food is often viewed through a strong spiritual lens, more so than anywhere else I know," he says.

Samuelsson, author of multiple cookbooks and the bestselling memoir *Yes, Chef* is the winner of multiple James Beard Awards and owns restaurants in New York and Sweden. He's been a UNICEF ambassador since 2000.

Chef Marcus Samuelsson's

HELGA'S MEATBALLS with LINGONBERRY PRESERVES & QUICK PICKLED CUCUMBERS

Some of my first memories in the kitchen were of my grandma Helga teaching me how to make her famous Swedish meatballs. They are such a traditional dish, but of course none are better than Mormor's. The time I spent with her in the kitchen is the single most important reason I wanted to be a chef—she taught me how to appreciate every ingredient and waste nothing. Something as simple as meatballs should be regarded with respect and care. In fact, I always make sure to have a version of this meatball in all of my restaurants. It's a nod to Helga and a love note to my family.

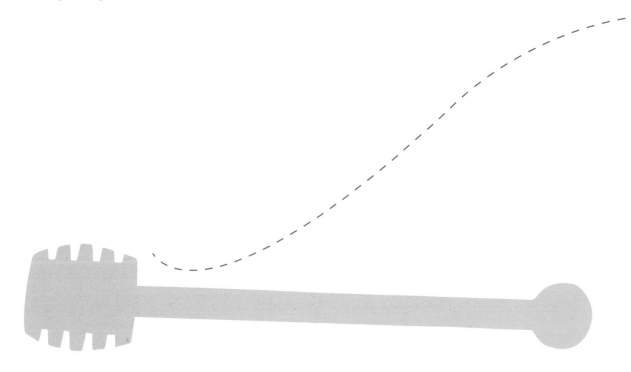

Meatballs:

½ cup dry breadcrumbs (50 g)

¼ cup heavy cream (60 ml)

2 tablespoons olive oil (30 ml)

1 medium red onion, finely chopped

½ pound ground chuck or sirloin (240 g)

½ pound ground veal (240 g)

½ pound ground pork (240 g)

2 tablespoons honey (30 ml)

1 large egg

Kosher salt

Freshly ground black pepper

3 tablespoons unsalted butter (42 g)

Sauce:

1 cup chicken stock (240 ml)

½ cup heavy cream (120 ml)

Lingonberry Preserves (recipe follows)

Quick Pickled Cucumbers (recipe follows)

1 To prepare the meatballs, combine the breadcrumbs and ¼ cup (60 ml) heavy cream in a small bowl, stirring with a fork until all the crumbs are moistened. Set aside.

2 Heat the oil in a small skillet over medium heat. Add the onion, and sauté for about 5 minutes, until softened. Remove from the heat.

3 In a large bowl, combine the ground beef, veal, pork, sautéed onion, honey, and egg, and mix well with your hands. Season with salt and pepper to taste. Add the breadcrumb-cream mixture, and mix well. With wet hands (to keep the mixture from sticking), shape the mixture into meatballs the size of a golf ball, placing them on a plate lightly moistened with water. You should have about 24 meatballs.

4 Melt the butter in a large skillet over medium-high heat. Add the meatballs, in batches if necessary, and cook, turning frequently, for about 7 minutes, until browned on all sides and cooked through. Remove from heat, transfer the meatballs to a plate, and discard all but 1 table-spoon (15 ml) of fat from the skillet.

5 To prepare the sauce, return the skillet to the heat, whisk in the stock, ½ cup (120 ml) cream, ¼ cup (80 g) preserves, and 2 tablespoons (30 ml) pickle juice from Quick Pickled Cucumbers; bring to a simmer. Season to taste with salt and pepper. Add the meatballs to the sauce, reduce the heat to medium, and simmer for about 5 minutes, until the sauce thickens slightly and the meatballs are heated through. Serve with Lingonberry Preserves and Quick Pickled Cucumbers.

1 English (hothouse) cucumber

1 tablespoon kosher salt (15 mL)

1½ cups water (360 mL)

½ cup white wine vinegar (120 mL)

1 cup sugar (200 g)

1 bay leaf

2 allspice berries

Quick Pickled Cucumbers

1 Slice the cucumber as thin as possible (use a mandoline or other vegetable slicer if you have one). Put the slices in a colander, toss them with the salt, and let stand for about 30 minutes.

2 Meanwhile, combine the water, vinegar, sugar, bay leaf, and allspice in a medium saucepan, and bring to a boil. Remove from heat, and let cool.

3 Rinse the salt off the cucumbers, and squeeze out as much moisture as possible. Put the cucumbers in a medium bowl, and add the pickling solution; the cucumbers should be completely covered by the brine. Cover and refrigerate for 3 to 6 hours before serving.

1 cup lingonberries (95 g)

2 cups sugar (400 g)

1 quart water (960 mL)

Lingonberry Preserves

1 Put ingredients in a pot. Bring to a boil. Reduce heat to low. Simmer until syrupy. Cool and serve.

Yield: about 2 cups (480 ml)

Aarón Sánchez

Mestizo Leawood / Kansas City, KS

The cooking of Aarón Sánchez captures the tension between memory and change that shapes the taste of generations. Sánchez's mother, Zarela Martinez, herself the daughter of a cookbook author, was born and raised in Mexico. After some time catering in Texas and cooking in New Orleans (with the legendary Paul Prudhomme), she opened Zarela in New York in 1987, pioneering authentic Mexican regional cooking in that city. When Sánchez, born in 1976, realized as a teen that he, too, needed to cook, he was already deeply schooled in the flavors of his mother's region, Chihuahua.

He remembers his mother's single-minded drive to find authentic flavors in New York: "I remember when we were living in the Upper West Side, we lived in a small apartment, and my mom was making mole. To make a proper mole you have to toast the chiles. I just remember the whole apartment filling with smoke and almost smoking out the entire building."

To this day, he says, "when I'm around that food, it means that I'm home."

Yet as an aspiring cook Sánchez wanted to make a home of his own. He turned to Nuevo Latino—the pan-Latin style of cooking that reflects the flow and mix of Mexican, Spanish, Caribbean, and Central and South American influences. Sánchez describes a continuous need to both expand beyond his roots and honor them. The menu at his Kansas City restaurant, Mestizo Leawood, opened in 2011, includes dishes like crisp pork belly with agave-chipotle glaze and cabbage slaw, and shaved Brussels sprouts with *chicharrones,*

cranberries, and Manchego cheese—both modern mash-ups rooted in Latin flavors. But there was also *sopa seca,* a traditional Mexican-style pasta with roasted tomato, chiles, and Cotija cheese that is one of Sánchez's signal memories of growing up.

Sánchez has a wide TV presence, notably as a sharply opinionated but encouraging judge on Food Network's popular *Chopped* and as a competitor on *Chopped All-Stars.* He's also a cookbook author.

¼ cup canola oil (60 mL)

1 cup small shaped pasta (100 g), such as melon seeds, orzo, or alphabets

½ cup Roasted Tomato-Chile de Árbol Salsa (120 g) (recipe follows)

2 cups chicken stock (480 mL) (low-sodium store-bought is fine)

1 tablespoon chopped fresh cilantro (15 mL)

A handful of shredded Cotija or queso fresco (preferably Cacique brand), Pecorino, Parmesan, or lightly salted feta

Chef Aarón Sánchez's

SOPA SECA

We didn't have a tradition of eating pasta, but we wanted that cheesy, tomatoey pasta feeling. I remember it simmering in the pot on the stove. It always seemed to be the same pot—it was old and had a few black marks up the side of it. I really wanted to remember that. And every time my mother made it, it was like the pot never ended; it was infinite. I could put as much cheese on it as I wanted to. My mother worked at night, so this was something she could make in the morning or in the afternoon while we were at school, and we would come back home and it would be there waiting for us.

1 Heat the oil in a Dutch oven or medium pot over medium-high heat until it ripples. Add the pasta and cook, stirring constantly, until the pasta is golden, about 3 minutes.

2 Scoop out and discard 2 tablespoons (30 ml) of the oil. Add the Roasted Tomato–Chile de Árbol Salsa, and cook 2 minutes, stirring constantly. Pour in the chicken stock, and let the liquid come to a simmer. Cover the pot, and cook, stirring once in a while, until the liquid is absorbed and the pasta is tender, about 20 minutes. Divide the pasta between 2 bowls, and garnish with the cilantro and cheese.

1 pound plum tomatoes (about 4, or 480 g)

3 to 6 chiles de árbol, depending on how spicy you like it

2 tablespoons olive oil (30 mL)

1 medium white onion, chopped

4 garlic cloves, crushed

½ cup chopped fresh cilantro (8 g)

1 teaspoon salt (5 mL)

½ teaspoon freshly ground black pepper (2 mL)

Roasted Tomato-Chile de Árbol Salsa

1 Preheat the broiler.

2 Put the tomatoes on a baking sheet, and broil until the tomatoes are nice and charred, 10 to 12 minutes. Take the tomatoes out, let them cool just until you can handle them, slip off the skins, and cut out the tough cores. Transfer the tomatoes to a big bowl (don't you dare forget the tomato juice that has leaked out and reduced to awesomeness on the baking sheet); then roughly chop them.

3 While the tomatoes are broiling, heat a dry skillet over medium heat, and toast the chiles (in batches, if necessary), flipping them over occasionally, until they just begin to smoke, about 5 minutes. Set them aside in a bowl. Put the olive oil, onion, and garlic in a saucepan over medium heat; cook, stirring occasionally, until the onion is soft, about 7 minutes. Add the toasted chiles, tomatoes, and 2 cups (480 ml) water; bring to a simmer, and cook for another 12 minutes, so the flavors come together. Let it cool a bit.

4 Carefully transfer the mixture to a blender. Add the cilantro, salt, and pepper, and puree until the mixture is very smooth. Strain the mixture through a medium-mesh sieve into a bowl. Serve at room temperature or slightly chilled. Store the salsa in the refrigerator, tightly covered, for up to a week, or in the freezer for a month.

Yield: 2 cups (480 g)

Suvir Saran

Devi / New York

Like many chefs, Suvir Saran, born in New Delhi, started down an entirely different path. He studied art in Bombay before leaving India in 1993 to attend the School of Visual Arts in New York, but once there, he found that cooking for friends revealed new possibilities. Saran started an Indian cuisine catering business, Rasoi, and eventually began teaching and consulting about food and health, an interest that continues today in his work with the Culinary Institute of America and the Harvard School of Public Health.

In the early 2000s, Manhattan, despite a large Indian population, was largely served by cookie-cutter Indian restaurants. That began to change when Saran cooked briefly at Amma—the menu included Indian street foods and a cauliflower-ketchup dish inspired by India's Chinese population—then opened Devi in 2004. That restaurant, Frank Bruni of the *New York Times* noted in a two-star review, featured food that was "varied, multidimensional, nimble, and surprising," including crispy fried okra dusted with ground mango peel, pomegranate seed, and toasted cumin; halibut cooked in banana leaves; and an ambitious tasting menu that featured calf brain mashed with green chili, quail eggs, and pickled ginger, served on bruschetta.

Saran branched into cookbooks, writing three: *Indian Home Cooking, American Masala,* and *Masala Farm,* the latter inspired by Saran's move to a 19th-century farm on 70 acres in upstate New York. He made a splash on season three of Bravo's *Top Chef Masters.* His work with the Culinary Institute of America and Harvard led to participation in the Menus of Change program, an annual summit devoted to the business of healthy, sustainable, and delicious food choices.

Chef Suvir Saran's

BIRBAL KEE KHITCHEREE

When craving comfort food, I most often dream of
khitcheree. This vegetarian one-pot meal of lentils, rice,
and vegetables is transported to another dimension via
multiple layers of spices—every bite is a new discovery of
tastes and textures. The dish includes *panch phoran*, a spice
blend of whole cumin, fennel, and the wonderfully exotic,
nutty flavor of nigella seeds that are gently fried in ghee
or clarified butter with coriander and tomatoes, and then
a second boost of spice from a ghee-bloomed blend of
more cumin, some cayenne, and oniony asafetida.

It is such an incredible dish that there is even a legend
behind it: Hundreds of years ago in mid-14th-century India,
Birbal, a court official of Emperor Akbar, made a *khitcheree*
that was so enchanting, the emperor decided to make Birbal
a Raja king! At our house, we like to say that if it's good
enough for Akbar and Birbal, it's good enough for you.
This dish is so lovely that I often serve it with nothing else
except for some raita and perhaps crispy *papadums* (very
thin crackers) on the side. Make the recipe a few times, and
then begin to play with the flavors and simplify it as you like.
I promise you won't be disappointed.

Topping:

6-8 cups peanut oil (1.4 to 2 L)

1 large red onion, halved and thinly sliced

¼ cup finely chopped fresh cilantro (4 g)

1 (2-inch) piece fresh gingerroot (5 cm), peeled and cut into very thin matchsticks

1 jalapeño, finely minced

1 tablespoon fresh lime juice (15 mL)

½ teaspoon garam masala (2 mL)

1 Heat the peanut oil in a large Dutch oven (enough to fill the pot to a 2-inch [5 cm] depth) over medium-high heat until it reaches 350° (180°C) on an instant-read thermometer. Add 1 sliced onion, and fry until crisp and browned, about 2 minutes, turning the onions occasionally. Use a slotted spoon or frying spider to transfer the onions to a paper towel–lined plate, and set aside. In a small bowl, combine the cilantro, ginger, jalapeño, and lime juice, and set aside.

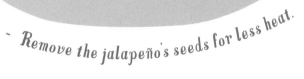

Remove the jalapeño's seeds for less heat.

Khitcheree:

1 cup split and hulled mung dal (200 g)

2 tablespoons ghee or clarified butter (28 g)

10 green cardamom pods

8 whole cloves

3 bay leaves

1 (2-inch) cinnamon stick (5 cm)

1 teaspoon panch phoran (5 mL) (Bengali five-spice)

¾ teaspoon turmeric (3 mL)

⅛ teaspoon asafetida (0.5 mL)

1 cup uncooked basmati rice (185 g)

½ medium head cauliflower (13 mm), cut into very small florets

1 medium red potato, cut into ½-inch pieces

4 medium carrots, peeled and finely chopped

7 cups water (1.7 L)

1 (10-ounce) bag frozen peas (285 g)

2 To prepare the khitcheree, place the mung dal in a large skillet over medium heat, and toast until it is fragrant and lightly golden, 3 to 5 minutes. Transfer the dal to a large plate, and set aside. Place 2 tablespoons ghee (28 g), cardamom, and next 6 ingredients (through ⅛ teaspoon asafetida [0.5 mL]) to the pan, and roast over medium heat until the spices are fragrant, about 2 minutes.

3 Add the rice, toasted dal, cauliflower, potatoes, and carrots; cook until the rice becomes translucent and the cauliflower sweats, 3 to 5 minutes, stirring often. Add 7 cups (1.7 L) water, increase heat to high, and bring to a boil. Add the peas; return to a boil. Reduce heat to medium-low, cover, and simmer 20 minutes.

First Tempering Oil:

2 tablespoons ghee or clarified butter (28 g)

½ teaspoon panch phoran (2 ml)

½ large red onion, halved and thinly sliced

1½ tablespoons kosher salt (22 ml)

2 teaspoons ground coriander (10 ml)

2 large tomatoes, finely diced

⅛ teaspoon cayenne pepper (0.5 ml)

3 cups water (720 ml)

Second Tempering Oil:

2 tablespoons ghee or clarified butter (28 g)

½ teaspoon cumin seeds (2 ml)

¼ teaspoon cayenne pepper (1 ml)

Dash of asafetida

4 While the rice and dal mixture cooks, make the first tempering oil. Heat 2 tablespoons ghee (28 g) and ½ teaspoon panch phoran (2 ml) in a large skillet over medium heat until the cumin in the panch phoran begins to brown, 2 to 3 minutes. Stir in ½ sliced onion and the salt; cook until the onions are browned around the edges and soft, about 10 minutes. If the onions begin to get too dark or stick to the pan bottom, splash the pan with a few tablespoons of water, and scrape up the browned bits. Stir in the coriander, and cook, stirring, for 2 minutes, and then stir in the tomatoes and ⅛ teaspoon cayenne. Cook until the tomatoes are jammy, 6 to 8 minutes, stirring occasionally. Turn off the heat, and set aside. Once the rice and dal are cooked, remove the lid and use a potato masher to smash the mixture until only a few carrots and peas remain whole (remove the whole or large spices while mashing if you like). Stir in the first tempering oil along with the remaining 3 cups water (720 ml). Return to a boil, and cook for 2 minutes. Turn off the heat.

5 Wipe out the pan from the first tempering oil, and heat 2 tablespoons (28 g) ghee for the second tempering oil over medium heat along with the cumin, ¼ teaspoon cayenne (1 ml), and a dash of asafetida; cook, stirring often, until the cumin begins to brown, about 2 minutes. Immediately stir the oil into the rice and dal mixture.

6 Divide the khitcheree among 6 bowls, and top with some of the ginger mixture, a dash of garam masala, and the fried onions, and serve.

Michael Solomonov

Zahav / Philadelphia

Chef Michael Solomonov has straddled two countries all his life, yet he never doubted where his roots lay. Though he grew up in Pittsburgh, Solomonov craves and cooks the food of Israel, the country where he was born and lived for several years before returning Stateside for college. This is the food of his ancestors, what Solomonov describes as "family-style dishes fresh from the grill with bountiful salads and sides to accompany them."

At Zahav, the menu, written in Hebrew and English, is divided into grilled items (*al ha'esh,* or "over the coals") like *branzino, kofte,* or veal-stuffed grape leaves; small plates; a bounty of salads (*salatim)*; and four kinds of hummus that trace their origins throughout the Middle East.

After a couple of semesters at college, Solomonov returned to Israel to reconnect with his homeland. He worked 12-hour shifts at a bakery making *laffah* and *burekas* before moving back to the U.S. for culinary school. A few years later, Philly chef Mark Vetri was ordering Middle Eastern herbs and spice blends at Solomonov's request, so the young line cook could use the ingredients in staff meals—a testing ground for his modern takes on Israeli classics. Solomonov opened Zahav in Philadelphia in 2008, and it was quickly rated by *Esquire* and *Philadelphia* magazines as the best new restaurant that year.

At Zahav, Solomonov cooks with nostalgia for a cuisine most Americans have yet to experience, with flavors both unexpected and comforting. He braises brisket in coffee, cardamom, and pomegranate because the smell reminds him of his mother's kitchen in their first home near Tel Aviv. Fewer dishes cry comfort more than matzo ball soup, yet Solomonov answers with a Yemeni version—traditionally a spare bowl of broth, chicken leg, and boiled potato made new with tender short ribs and pickled onion. At Zahav, potatoes are crisped in *schmaltz*, the chicken-y fat that has recently returned to fashion among some U.S. chefs.

Solomonov won a James Beard Award for Best Chef: Mid-Atlantic in 2011 and was recognized by *Food & Wine* as a "top empire builder" in 2012 for Zahav, Percy Street Barbecue, and Federal Donuts ("Coffee. Donuts. Chicken."), which he also co-owns. Solomonov continues to make frequent visits to Israel with his staff and family.

Chef Michael Solomonov's

HUMMUS-MASBACHA

We serve four different kinds of hummus, all with fresh *laffah* bread from our oven. It whets the appetite and sets the stage for a hearty feast—with plenty of passing and sharing and no one being too shy to mop up the last contents of any bowl with a little of that heavenly bread. After sharing a bowl of homemade hummus, it's hard to imagine anything but a raucous, warm, convivial meal together.

1 pound dry chickpeas (480 g)

1 tablespoon baking soda (15 ml)

1 whole head of garlic with the skin on, plus 1 peeled garlic clove

2 cups unhulled sesame paste (480 g)

½ cup grapeseed oil (120 ml)

½ cup freshly squeezed lemon juice (120 ml)

Kosher salt to taste

Ground cumin to taste

¾ cup extra-virgin olive oil (180 ml) (preferably from Turkey or Israel)

¼ cup chopped fresh Italian parsley (15 g)

1   To make hummus, soak chickpeas and baking soda with at least double their volume of water for 18 hours in refrigerator. Drain the chickpeas, and rinse thoroughly in cold water. Place the chickpeas in a large pot with whole head of garlic, and cover with water. Over high heat, bring water to a boil; reduce the heat to low, and simmer chickpeas until very tender, approximately 3 hours. Drain chickpeas, reserving 1 cup (240 ml) of the cooking liquid. Discard garlic bulb.

2   In the bowl of a food processor, add 1½ cups (360 g) sesame paste and all but 1 cup (164 g) cooked chickpeas. Puree the mixture with grapeseed oil and ¼ cup (60 ml) lemon juice. Add enough reserved cooking liquid to achieve a smooth, creamy consistency. Season to taste with kosher salt and ground cumin.

3   To make tehina, combine the remaining ¼ cup (60 ml) lemon juice and ½ cup (120 g) sesame paste with garlic clove and ½ cup (120 ml) warm water in a blender. Blend at high speed until smooth; add ½ cup (120 ml) olive oil. If the puree is too tight, adjust the consistency with additional warm water. Season to taste with kosher salt and ground cumin.

4   To serve, spoon hummus into a large, shallow bowl, creating a well in the center of the hummus. In a mixing bowl, toss the reserved chickpeas with tehina. Spoon dressed chickpeas into the well. Garnish with chopped parsley and remaining olive oil. Serve immediately.

Frank Stitt

Highlands Bar and Grill / Birmingham, AL

Frank Stitt is recognized by many chefs as the god-father of new Southern cooking, appreciated equally for his love of regional traditions, his kitchen precision, and his restaurant savvy. A true Southerner by birth—he grew up in Cullman, Alabama, not far north of Birmingham—Stitt spent a summer in Europe after high school, began college in Massachusetts, and then transferred to Berkeley to study philosophy in the mid-1970s. Berkeley was ground zero for the exploding California food scene, and Stitt was fascinated by the food writing of Richard Olney and Elizabeth David—and eventually by the idea of a life in cooking. After several failed attempts to land a gig apprenticing at local restaurants, he found a taker and soon ended up in the kitchen of Alice Waters at Chez Panisse. Through Waters, he met Julia Child, Jeremiah Tower, and Simone Beck and found a position assisting Olney, who was living in Provence and compiling a multivolume Time-Life series on cooking.

After leaving France, Stitt worked in the Caribbean before returning to Alabama to serve as a chef in a hotel and plot the launch of his first restaurant. Local banks were not impressed, so he approached friends and family. Highlands Bar and Grill opened in November 1982. There, Stitt dazzled diners with Southern dishes that retained their soul but were dressed up with French technique and refinement. The restaurant also became regionally important for its emphasis on sourcing foods from area farms. Today, Highlands remains the jewel of the Birmingham dining scene, offering dishes like Poached Farm Egg with House-Cured Bacon, Creamy Grits, and Ham Hock Jus, and Beef Cheek with Crowder Peas, Potato Puree, and Tomato Relish.

In 1988, Stitt opened the Italian-tilting Bottega, also in Birmingham. He later expanded his empire with two more casual eateries, Bottega Café and Chez Fonfon, a deftly executed French bistro.

Stitt was named Best Chef: Southeast in 2001 by the James Beard Foundation and was a 2008 finalist for the Foundation's Outstanding Chef award. He has also been recognized with a Lifetime Achievement Award from the Southern Foodways Alliance. His first cookbook, *Frank Stitt's Southern Table,* was a bestseller. Another book, *Bottega Favorita,* followed.

Chef Frank Stitt's

AUTUMN BEET SALAD with SPICED PECANS, PEARS & FOURME D'AMBERT

Each ingredient in this satisfying and healthy dish brings back special memories of growing up in Cullman, Alabama. Since I was a child, pears have been a favorite fruit of mine. We had a pear tree in our backyard, and I loved the crunchy, sweet taste of a pear right off the branch (as well as my mother's pear preserves).

My mother and I would savor a beet salad with vinegar, horseradish, and sour cream back when most thought we were probably Communists because we loved the strange purple vegetable. Small lardons, or slabs of bacon, add richness to the salad and are especially good in combination with the blue cheese, pecans, pears, and beets.

Beets:

4 small beets, stems trimmed, gently washed

Kosher salt and freshly ground black pepper

1 teaspoon extra-virgin olive oil (5 ml)

Splash of red wine vinegar

¼-pound slab bacon (120 g), cut into 1-inch lardons (2.5 cm)

Salad:

Scant 3 cups mixed lettuce (175 g), such as baby romaine, Lolla Rosso, and frisée, trimmed if necessary, washed and dried

Kosher salt and freshly ground black pepper to taste

3 to 4 tablespoons Sherry Vinaigrette (45 to 60 ml) (recipe follows)

2 Bartlett pears, quartered, cored, and thinly sliced lengthwise

½ cup Spiced Pecans (60 g) (recipe follows)

Scant ¼ pound Fourme d'Ambert (about 120 g) or other blue cheese, such as Roquefort or Stilton, cut into 4 wedges

1 Preheat the oven to 350° (180°C).

2 Place the beets on a square of foil, season with salt and pepper, and drizzle with the olive oil and the vinegar. Wrap them in the foil and bake until tender, 45 to 60 minutes. Allow them to cool; then peel and cut each beet into eighths.

3 Place the bacon lardons in a large pan, and cook over medium heat until just rendered and barely crisp, about 4 minutes. Set aside and keep warm.

4 In a medium bowl, toss the mixed greens with the salt, pepper, and vinaigrette to taste.

5 Place a mound of salad on each plate. Scatter the beets, pears, lardons, and pecans around, and arrange a wedge of cheese on each plate.

½ shallot, finely minced

4 thyme sprigs, leaves removed

Kosher salt and freshly ground black pepper to taste

2 tablespoons sherry vinegar (30 mL)

6 tablespoons extra-virgin olive oil (90 mL)

Sherry Vinaigrette

1 In a small bowl, combine the shallot, thyme, and a good pinch each of salt and pepper. Add the sherry vinegar, and let macerate for 10 minutes.

2 Whisk in the olive oil in a slow, steady stream. Taste and adjust the seasoning. (The vinaigrette can be refrigerated for up to 5 days.)

Yield: ½ cup (120 ml)

---

4 cups pecan halves (440 g)

1½ teaspoons kosher salt (7 mL)

Pinch of freshly ground black pepper (0.3 mL)

¼ teaspoon cayenne pepper (1 mL)

1 heaping teaspoon dark brown sugar (5 mL)

1 heaping tablespoon freshly chopped rosemary leaves (15 mL)

1 tablespoon melted butter (15 mL)

2 tablespoons olive oil (30 mL)

Spiced Pecans

1 Preheat the oven to 350° (180°C).

2 Place the pecans on a baking sheet and bake for 15 minutes. Remove from the oven. Season the pecans with the salt, pepper, cayenne, sugar, rosemary, butter, and olive oil. Toss together until the pecans are thoroughly coated. Return the pecans to the oven for another 2 to 3 minutes, until toasted and fragrant, but be careful not to overcook them.

Yield: 4 cups (490 g)

Curtis Stone

Top Chef Masters | Bravo

Australian-born Curtis Stone left business school in Melbourne to cook locally before making his way to the U.K., where he offered to work for free in the Michelin-starred kitchens of Marco Pierre White and remained, rising in those competitive ranks, for more than four years. But TV beckoned, first in the U.K., then in Australia, then in America, where Stone was given his own series, *Take Home Chef*, in 2006. Since then, his television work has been prodigious. He has appeared on *The Biggest Loser*, co-hosted *America's Next Great Restaurant*, and hosted Bravo's *Top Chef Masters* starting in season three.

Stone is known for his entrepreneurial bent—he has a large cookware line—and his media sparkle, promoting fresh, simple everyday cooking to a global audience. His fifth cookbook, *What's For Dinner? Delicious Recipes for a Busy Life*, published in 2013, was a *New York Times* bestseller.

Chef Curtis Stone's

GRILLED LOBSTER with SWEET CORN BUTTER & BACON MARMALADE

Grilling is a way of life in Australia. We do it all summer long. Growing up close to the ocean, we naturally grill a lot of seafood, including lobster, which is always a show-stopper. In this variation I've used corn butter, which is sweet, creamy, and lighter than straight butter. It's perfect for a summer night.

Corn Butter:

3 cups fresh corn kernels (500 g) (cut from 4 large ears yellow corn)

1 tablespoon fresh thyme leaves (15 mL), finely chopped

8 tablespoons (1 stick) salted butter (112 g), cut into ½-inch pieces, softened (13 mm)

Bacon Marmalade:

5 slices bacon, cut into ½-inch pieces (13 mm)

½ cup chopped shallots (85 g)

2 teaspoons finely chopped fresh thyme (10 mL)

½ cup sherry vinegar (120 mL)

1 cup dry sherry (240 mL)

¼ cup extra-virgin olive oil (60 mL)

Kosher salt and freshly ground black pepper

1 To make the corn butter, run the corn kernels through an electric juicer to extract the corn juice; discard the solids. You should get at least 1½ cups (360 ml) of corn juice. Or, if you don't have a juicer, puree the kernels in a blender. Strain the juice through a fine-mesh sieve set over a bowl, pressing hard on the solids to extract all the juice.

2 In a small, heavy nonaluminum saucepan, bring the corn juice to a boil over medium heat, whisking constantly; then whisk for about 10 minutes or until it thickens to a pudding-like consistency (the natural starch in the corn will cause the juice to thicken). Transfer to a small bowl.

3 Whisk 1 tablespoon (15 ml) thyme into the corn juice. Whisk in the butter, a few pieces at a time. Press a sheet of plastic wrap on the surface of the butter, and let cool to room temperature.

4 To make the bacon marmalade, heat a large, heavy saucepan over medium-high heat. Add the bacon, and cook, stirring occasionally, about 5 minutes or until it is nearly crisp. Add the shallots and 2 teaspoons thyme (10 ml), and sauté about 2 minutes or until the shallots are tender. Add the vinegar, and cook about 5 minutes or until reduced by half. Add the sherry, and cook about 10 minutes or until reduced by half. Transfer to a small bowl and set aside to cool slightly; then stir in the extra-virgin olive oil, and season to taste with salt and pepper. Set aside at room temperature for up to 2 hours.

Lobsters:

6 live Maine lobsters (1½ pounds, or 720 g each)

1 tablespoon olive oil (15 mL)

3 large ears yellow corn, husked and cut in half

Kosher salt

Chopped fresh chives for garnish

5 Bring a large pot of salted water to a boil over high heat. Add 1 lobster, and immediately turn off the heat. Let the lobster cook gently in the hot water for 3 minutes. The lobster will be medium-rare at this point, which is what you want, since it will be grilled later. Remove the lobster from the hot water, and immediately place it in a large bowl of ice water to cool. Repeat with the remaining 5 lobsters, returning the water to a boil before placing each lobster in the water. Once they are cool, drain the lobsters.

6 Remove the claws from the lobsters. Using a very sharp chef's knife, cut the lobster bodies lengthwise in half; remove and discard the intestines.

7 Prepare an outdoor grill for high cooking over direct heat.

8 Brush the lobster tail meat generously with some of the corn but-ter. Grill the lobster halves, cut side down, with the claws for about 4 minutes, or until grill marks appear on the meat; then turn over the lobster halves and claws, and cook for about 2 minutes longer, until cooked through. Meanwhile, lightly oil the ears of corn, season with salt, and grill, turning occasionally, for about 8 minutes or until slightly charred.

9 To serve, transfer the corn and lobster to 6 dinner plates or platters. Spoon more corn butter and some bacon marmalade over the lobster meat. Garnish with the chives. Serve the remaining corn butter and bacon marmalade alongside.

Vikram Sunderam

Rasika / Washington, D.C.

Chef Vikram Sunderam says he has much to learn about Indian cuisine—a claim his fans would have found absurd 20 years ago, let alone today, when he is the most celebrated Indian chef in Washington, D.C. Sunderam grew up in Bombay, his mother a fine cook. After graduating from a rigorous culinary program, he joined the renowned Taj hotel group in 1985 and advanced to head chef. The company brought Sunderam to London, where he eventually became executive chef at Bombay Brasserie. In 2005, restaurateur Ashok Bajaj convinced Sunderam to helm Rasika in Washington D.C.'s Penn Quarter, and it's now a constant contender for best area restaurant. Despite constant praise from critics, a lifetime of exposure and training, and multiple James Beard nominations, Sunderam says he is still learning, referencing, asking questions.

Traditional Indian food with a modern edge has been done before, but Sunderam isn't capitalizing on a trend. His focus is purely on flavor, the meaning of *rasika* in Sanskrit. This is reflected in a menu that often reads like the spare haikus of an ultramodern restaurant in the Eleven Madison Park vein. Honey Ginger Scallops is described simply as "scallops/burnt garlic/red pepper," Tandoori Trout as "chili flakes/Kaffir lime/lemon pickle." These simple descriptions also apply to the house-made chutneys, curries, tandoori, and *sigri* (Indian barbeque), barely hinting at the complexity of the plated foods. Sunderam lets the food speak for itself, which it does, extravagantly.

Bajaj and Sunderam opened Rasika West End in March 2012. The two restaurants complement rather than copy each other, giving Sunderam a chance to express his traditional roots at one while trying a more contemporary style at the other.

Chef Vikram Sunderam's

AVOCADO-BANANA CHAAT

Chaat refers to savory dishes sold in street-side stalls throughout India. There are many variations, including potatoes, chickpeas, samosas, chicken, and *paneer*, to name a few. They are typically savory, sweet, tangy, salty, spicy, and often crunchy. This makes them perfect for enjoying at the beginning of the meal to awaken and enhance the palate. At Rasika we have created a dish incorporating avocados and bananas. The nutty and creamy texture of the avocado complements the tangy and savory flavor of the dish.

½ cup chopped onion (56 g)

½ cup chopped tomato (80 g)

2 tablespoons chopped fresh cilantro (30 mL)

1 teaspoon roasted cumin powder (5 mL)

½ teaspoon red chili powder (2 mL)

¼ teaspoon black salt (1 mL)

¼ cup Tamarind Chutney (65 g) (recipe follows)

2 ripe firm avocados, cut into ¼-inch pieces (6 mm)

2 ripe firm bananas, cut into quarters

Salt

Freshly ground black pepper

Chopped fresh cilantro

1 Combine the first 7 ingredients in a serving bowl. Arrange on top of avocado.

2 Sear the bananas cut sides down, in a skillet over medium heat. Season with salt and pepper. Arrange 2 banana pieces on each plate. Garnish with cilantro. Serve cold.

1 pound tamarind (480 g)

½ pound pitted dates (240 g)

1 ounce minced peeled fresh ginger (28 g)

1 ounce minced garlic (28 g)

2 ounces jiggery (57 g)

2 ounces sugar (57 g)

5 whole red chilies

4 bay leaves

1 tablespoon fennel seeds (15 mL)

1 teaspoon roasted cumin powder (5 mL)

1 teaspoon red chili powder (5 mL)

½ teaspoon black salt (2 mL)

Salt

Tamarind Chutney

1 Place the first 9 ingredients in a heavy saucepan. Add enough water to cover the ingredients. Bring to a boil; reduce heat, and simmer until the dates and tamarind are soft. Strain tamarind mixture through a fine-mesh sieve over a bowl. Season the extract with the roasted cumin powder, red chili powder, black salt, and salt. Refrigerate.

Ming Tsai

Blue Ginger / Wellesley, MA

Ming Tsai remembers the day he first cooked for someone else, at age 10. It was fried rice, a bit oily, but enjoyed by the surprise guests. His conclusion: "I could make people happy through food: How cool was that?"

Tsai comes from a family made happy through food. His father and mother, both born in Beijing, met in New Haven, Connecticut, at the dinner table of his grandfather's home. Tsai grew up in Dayton, Ohio, where his love of cooking and eating was passed on and nurtured by his parents as he worked alongside them at their family-owned restaurant, Mandarin Kitchen.

A food career seemed natural, but before that, in the family tradition, some serious schooling: Phillips Academy in Andover, then Yale for a degree in mechanical engineering. While in college, Tsai spent summers at Le Cordon Bleu cooking school in Paris. After graduating from Yale, he moved to Paris and trained under pastry chef Pierre Hermé. He then trained in Osaka, Japan, with sushi master Kobayashi. Thus French and Japanese techniques framed his love of Chinese cooking, and these influences persist in the menus of his restaurants.

Returning to the United States, Tsai got a master's in hotel administration and hospitality management before opening Blue Ginger in Wellesley, Massachusetts, in 1998. The restaurant garnered three stars in its first year from *The Boston Globe* and a Best New Restaurant nod from *Boston Magazine.* Today it serves dishes like foie gras–shiitake *shumai* in Sauternes-shallot broth; grilled marinated top sirloin with Szechwan glaze and crispy chow mein salad; and a version of coq au vin with a ginger-plum wine reduction. In 2002, he won the James Beard Award for Best Chef: Northeast and in 2013 opened a second restaurant, Blue Dragon, an "Asian gastropub" in Boston.

From the start, Tsai had television in his sights. He debuted as Emmy-winning host of *East Meets West with Ming Tsai* in 1998. His public television series, *Simply Ming,* received two Emmy nominations. He is also the author of five cookbooks, including *Blue Ginger: East Meets West Cooking with Ming Tsai* and *Simply Ming.*

Tsai now passes his family's food philosophy on to his two kids. He sums up the approach with a question: "*Chi le ma?* (have you eaten?) In my family, this is the proper greeting when you see friends or family. We are not as concerned about how you are, but whether you are hungry. All present need an opportunity to eat together as soon as possible."

Chef Ming Tsai's

EIGHT-TREASURE RICE

This dish has a mixed pedigree. It's based partly on eight-treasure rice, a traditional Chinese pudding whose treasures include lotus seeds, dates, and red beans. Its other forebear is *jong zi*, a delicious dim sum made with glutinous rice and pork. I've taken the idea of a savory yet meatless rice dish filled with good things and run with it, creating a great fried rice that's truly a meal-in-one. This is a dish that meat lovers as well as the meat-averse will devour.

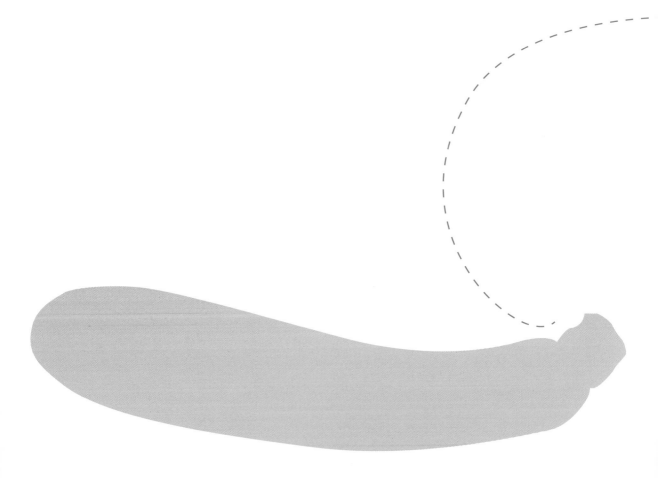

5 tablespoons canola oil (75 mL)

4 large eggs, beaten

Kosher salt

1 tablespoon minced garlic (15 mL)

1 tablespoon minced ginger (15 mL)

1 serrano chile, minced

1 large zucchini, diced

1 bunch scallions, white and green parts, thinly sliced, 1 tablespoon of the greens reserved for garnish (15 mL)

Freshly ground black pepper

⅓ pound shiitake mushrooms (160 g), stemmed and cut into ⅛-inch slices (3 mm)

2 tablespoons wheat-free tamari (30 mL)

1 cup shelled edamame (120 g)

7 cups cooked and cooled 50-50 House Steamed Rice (1.2 kg) (recipe follows)

2 tablespoons toasted sesame seeds (30 mL)

1 Line a large plate with paper towels. Heat a wok over high heat. Add 4 tablespoons (60 ml) oil, and swirl to coat. When the oil is hot, add the eggs and season with salt. When the eggs puff, stir vigorously; then transfer the eggs to the paper towels to drain.

2 Add the remaining 1 tablespoon oil (15 ml) to the wok, swirl to coat, and heat over high heat. When the oil is hot, add the garlic, ginger, and chile, and stir-fry until aromatic, about 30 seconds. Lower the heat to medium-high, add the zucchini and all but the reserved 1 tablespoon (15 ml) scallions, and stir-fry until slightly softened, about 1 minute. Season with salt and pepper. Add the shiitakes and tamari, and stir-fry until soft, about 2 minutes. Add the edamame and eggs. Stir to break up the eggs; then add the rice. Stir until heated through, about 2 minutes. Adjust the seasoning with salt and pepper.

3 Transfer to a large serving platter; garnish with the reserved scallion greens and the sesame seeds.

1½ cups uncooked brown rice (185 g)

1½ cups uncooked white rice (185 g)

50-50 House Steamed Rice

1 Rinse brown rice, and let soak in fresh cold water to cover for about 1 hour.

2 In the meantime, rinse the white rice by placing it in a bowl filled with water and stirring by hand. Drain and repeat until the water in the bowl is clear.

3 Add both brown and white rice to a saucepan. Flatten the rice with your palm and, without removing your hand, add water until it touches the highest knuckle of your middle finger.

4 Cover and boil over high heat for 10 minutes. Reduce the heat to medium, and simmer 30 minutes. Turn off the heat and let the rice stand, covered, to plump, 20 minutes. Stir gently and serve.

Yield: 4 servings

Norman Van Aken

Tuyo / Miami

He was born in the Midwest—Diamond Lake, Illinois, to be exact—but Norman Van Aken's heart belongs to Key West.

"I am neither Southern nor Cuban but I like to consider myself a 'multitude,'" he wrote in his most recent cookbook, *My Key West Kitchen,* co-written with his son, Justin. "We are in the clasp of different cultures but slightly askew, afloat here in the Gulfstream off Florida. Yet the spirit of Key West is in the fish my son and I both prize, the lard melting in cast-iron pans, the sweet fruits that hang heavy from our trees, the beans we simmer, the greens we treasure."

It was 1973, when Van Aken was sitting in "a shack of a restaurant" with turtle steak and a classic Latin meat dish called *ropa vieja* on the menu, that a goateed fellow named "Bud Man" offered him a job cooking ribs, Brunswick stew, and chowder in an all-night, open-air joint called The Midget.

Van Aken had some experience cooking back home at Tom & Jerry's Fireside Inn. But his work at The Midget marked the beginning of a 40-year journey in the varied and eccentric kitchen habits of Key West. The self-schooled Van Aken relishes the "crazy matrix of foods" he experienced while learning the flavors of the American South, the Bahamas, and Cuba.

He has been called the founding father of New World cuisine and credited for propelling the concept of fusion in American restaurant kitchens (he introduced a paper on the subject in 1988). He's published five cookbooks and a memoir (*No Experience Necessary*), and his storytelling is world-class, which may explain why his late dear friend and fellow chef Charlie Trotter referred to him as "the Walt Whitman of American cuisine."

Van Aken has won many awards, including Best Chef: Southeast from the James Beard Foundation. He hosts a radio show called *A Word on Food* and is the chef and director of restaurants at The Miami Culinary Institute and its Tuyo restaurant, well as the chef and co-owner of Norman's at The Ritz-Carlton, Orlando, Grande Lakes.

Chef Norman Van Aken's

CARAMELIZED PLANTAIN SOUP with SMOKED HAM & SOUR CREAM

Shortly after moving to Key West in the early 1970s, I got some temporary work helping some carpenter buddies of mine rebuild some of the tottering, but still beautiful, wooden houses on the island. When the "hunger bell" rang we'd go to a place on Duval Street for meals that included *mojo* pork, *palomilla* steaks, fish stews, various bean soups, and, of course, sweet, honey-hued, chewy-soft, heavenly fried plantains. Plantains were the first exotic food that I tried when I moved to Key West that just blew me away. At first I didn't know what I was doing when I cooked them at home. I had no *abuela* (grandmother) coaxing me to "let them ripen, chico! Let them turn almost black if you want them to taste the way you like them in the cafés."

The green ones are good for chips, the mottled ones for boiling, and the black or *maduro* ones are the ones for this rich and nurturing soup.

¼ cup plus 1 tablespoon pure olive oil (75 mL)

2 tablespoons unsalted butter (28 g)

2 very ripe plantains, skinned and cut into ½-inch-thick slices (13 mm)

Dash (0.5 mL) each of salt, sugar, and cayenne pepper

½ teaspoon ground turmeric (2 mL)

2 leeks, cleaned and finely diced, white parts only

1 large carrot, trimmed, peeled, and finely diced

1 sweet onion, finely diced

3 garlic cloves, thinly sliced

1 Scotch bonnet chile, stemmed, seeded, and minced

1 cup fresh orange juice (240 mL)

4 cups chicken stock (960 mL)

2 cups heavy cream (480 mL)

Kosher salt and freshly ground black pepper

½ cup cooked ham (56 g), diced or shredded

½ cup sour cream (115 g)

Chopped fresh parsley (optional)

1 Add the oil and butter to a large saucepan, and heat over medium-high heat. Add the plantains; season with salt, sugar, and cayenne. Cook, stirring occasionally, until the plantains have browned, about 10 minutes. Stir in the turmeric, leeks, carrot, onion, garlic, and chile pepper, and cook until the vegetables are nicely caramelized, about 10 minutes. Stir in the orange juice, and cook for 2 minutes. Stir in the chicken stock, and bring to a boil.

2 Reduce the heat to a high simmer, and cook the soup for about 12 minutes or until the orange juice is reduced by half. Stir in the heavy cream, turn up the heat, and reduce the soup for about 5 minutes, until it reaches a creamy consistency. Remove from the heat. Season to taste. Keep warm. Just before serving, stir the ham into the soup to warm it up. Ladle the soup into cups or bowls, and dollop with sour cream. Garnish with parsley, if desired.

Alice Waters

Chez Panisse / Berkeley, CA

Alice Waters is simply the most influential chef of postwar 20th-century America, still going strong more than 40 years after opening Berkeley's Chez Panisse in 1971. Chez Panisse, through the simplicity and directness of its food, promoted the idea that a restaurant should interact with a community of farmers, ranchers, and artisans whose products evoke a deep connection to soil and craft. If you eat locally grown heirloom rice at Husk in Charleston or rare tomatoes in any hip Brooklyn café, give a nod to Alice Waters.

The root culinary influence, especially in the early days, was French. As Waters, born in 1944, told *OnlineChef,* her market-fresh inspiration came from living in France at the age of 19: "My home was on the other side of a farmers market, and I walked through that market every day on my way to school. I think I just absorbed that love of fresh ingredients through osmosis. When I came back to California, I wanted those same foodstuffs here."

Farm-to-table did not come easy in 1970s America, however, and the restaurant struggled." It took a long time to develop a local farming system to produce and support fresh, local ingredients," she recalls.

Chez Panisse turned Waters into an internationally known chef, while her restaurant turned out future stars like Jeremiah Tower, Paul Bertolli, Mark Miller, and Jonathan Waxman. But the dean of California cuisine would not pursue the model followed by so many chefs since: a string of trademarked restaurants across the country or around the world. Chez Panisse and the café above it remain Waters's only restaurants. Her interests extend far beyond, however.

In 1996, she created The Edible Schoolyard at Berkeley's Martin Luther King Jr. Middle School: a 1-acre garden with adjacent kitchen-classroom, and an "eco-gastronomic" curriculum—the whole package a model for a movement to bring kids closer to the idea of good food. The Edible Schoolyard has been nationally recognized for integrating gardening, cooking, and school lunches into the core academic curriculum. Waters established the Chez Panisse Foundation in 1996 to support the Schoolyard.

Waters is vice president of Slow Food International, a nonprofit organization that promotes and celebrates local artisanal food traditions and has 100,000 members in more than 150 countries. She is the author of 12 books, including *The Art of Simple Food: Notes, Lessons, and Recipes from a Delicious Revolution.*

Chef Alice Waters's

GRILLED CORN on the COB

When I was growing up in New Jersey, my family, like so many people at the time, had a victory garden. Looking back on it, that garden had a deep impact on us. Not only did it symbolically connect us to the war effort and to everyone else, but we were, as a family, truly able to feed ourselves from that garden. We couldn't afford to eat out very much, and that victory garden literally sustained us. Corn was the only vegetable I really liked when I was little, and I loved it picked fresh from our garden and simply grilled. This was one of my first lessons in ripeness, sweetness, and season-ality and what a difference it can make. Grilling corn is the easiest thing in the world, and a steaming ear of sweet corn on the cob slathered with butter is the perfect emblem of summer and local farms.

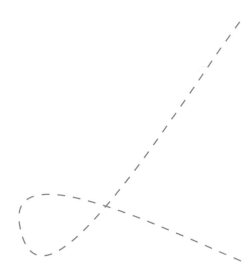

4 ears sweet corn, unshucked

Salt and freshly ground black pepper to taste

Ground dried ancho chiles (optional)

Lime wedges (optional)

Fresh parsley, savory, or scallions (optional)

Butter or olive oil

Chez Panisse Vegetables by Alice Waters, 1996, HarperCollins

1 Prepare a grill over a medium to medium-hot fire.

2 Peel back the husks of the corn, leaving them connected at the base of each ear, and remove all silk. Season corn with salt and pepper and a little chile or herbs; brush with butter or oil, and sprinkle with a little water. Rewrap the ears in their husks to protect them, and grill over a medium to medium-hot fire, turning now and then, for about 10 minutes. You can serve corn on the cob with butter, salt, lime wedges, and ground dried ancho chiles, or with a compound butter made of softened butter, chopped parsley, chopped savory, and finely sliced scallions.

To grind dried ancho chiles, first remove their seeds and veins, and then pulverize the chiles in a mortar and pestle or in a spice grinder.

Geoffrey Zakarian

The Lambs Club / New York

Geoffrey Zakarian is a quintessentially urban American chef with deep cooking chops who has played a major role in the rehabilitation and return to fashion of the New York hotel restaurant. Zakarian trained at the Culinary Institute of America in Hyde Park, New York before apprenticing under Alain Sailhac and then Daniel Boulud in the ferociously busy kitchen of Le Cirque. Over five years—1982 to 1987—he rose to chef de cuisine at Le Cirque, rooting him permanently in the finest points of French technique. During these years, he also *staged* in top French restaurants abroad.

In 1988, after a brief turn at 21 Club, Zakarian became executive chef at 44 in the hipster-hotbed Royalton hotel, a restaurant made buzzy by the likes of Tina Brown in the early 1990s. In 1995, Zakarian opened the Blue Door at the scene-defining Delano Hotel in South Beach. Two years later he was executive chef at Patroon, earning three *New York Times* stars, then opened his own restaurant, Town, in a Midtown hotel. The food at Town, also earning three stars from the *Times*, was the picture of new American refinement, as it would be downtown at Country and, in 2010, in the polished Empire Deco confines of The Lambs Club in the Chatwal Hotel.

Along the way, television beckoned, and Zakarian's smooth style and competitive streak moved him from popular judge on *Chopped* to winning Iron Chef laurels on *The Next Iron Chef: Super Chefs.*

Zakarian credits his staying power in part to an enduring love of restaurants. "I still dream of a small restaurant I visited in Provence decades ago that taught me the balance of simple flavors and the art of heartfelt hospitality," he says. "Still today, I dine out all the time, first because I love it, but secondly because, as a chef, you need to see restaurants from the dining room perspective, not just from the kitchen."

Chef Geoffrey Zakarian's

BRAISED LAMB SHANKS

I love lamb of any kind. Being Middle Eastern, we had a bounty in my house growing up, but usually the tougher cuts, which we braised for long hours till meltingly tender and falling off the bone. This recipe does exactly that, albeit with a slightly elevated cut of lamb.

I honed this recipe for the opening of the Blue Door restaurant at the Delano Hotel. But the idea was planted years ago when I had *gigot de sept heures* (seven-hour lamb) in France; it was so tender that they served it without a knife. The crucial flavor-building step here is to create a spice rub and allow the lamb to marinate well in advance.

The rest of the procedure involves straightforward braising: It takes a long time, but once you've put the pan in the oven, you leave it alone and you can go about your other business. (In fact, it's best not to disturb the shanks much at all.) Once you've reduced the braising liquid to a sauce—another simple procedure that leaves you free to make other preparations—the meal is ready to serve. Be sure to wash it down with a bottle of hearty Rhône red or some equivalent wine.

3 tablespoons ground cumin (45 mL)

3 tablespoons ground coriander (45 mL)

2 tablespoons Madras curry powder (30 mL)

2 tablespoons minced fresh rosemary (30 mL)

2 tablespoons minced fresh thyme (30 mL)

2 tablespoons minced garlic (30 mL)

1 tablespoon coarsely ground black pepper (15 mL), plus more to taste

½ cup plus 2 tablespoons extra-virgin olive oil (150 mL)

1 tablespoon kosher salt (15 mL), plus more to taste

6 lamb shanks (1 to 1¼ pounds each), (480 to 600 g) excess fat trimmed

2 stalks celery, coarsely chopped

1 large yellow onion, coarsely chopped

1 large carrot, coarsely chopped

1 cup dry white wine (240 mL)

2 quarts low-sodium canned chicken stock (1.9 L)

1 To marinate the lamb shanks, place the first 7 ingredients in a small mixing bowl, and stir to combine well. Stir in 6 tablespoons (90 mL) of the oil to make a paste. Season the paste with 1 tablespoon salt (15 mL). Rub the lamb shanks with the spice rub, place them in a dish, and cover with plastic wrap (or in place a large, resealable plastic bag), and refrigerate overnight.

2 Preheat oven to 350° (180°C).

3 Wipe the paste from the shanks with a paper towel, and discard. Heat 2 tablespoons of the oil (30 mL) in a large, ovenproof skillet over medium heat. (Choose a pan that is large enough to hold the shanks in a single snug layer, or use a separate large roasting pan for braising.) Working in batches if necessary, brown the shanks on all sides, about 20 minutes. Wipe out the skillet (it is important to discard any burned spices). Add the remaining 2 tablespoons oil (30 mL) with the celery, onion, and carrot; cook over medium heat until the vegetables begin to soften and brown, about 12 minutes. Return the shanks to the pan, add the wine, and simmer until the pan is almost dry, about 8 minutes. Add the stock, and bring to a simmer. Cover the pan, and place it in the oven at 350° (180°C) to braise for 1 hour. (If using a separate roasting pan, transfer all contents before placing in oven.) Turn the shanks, and cook until the lamb is very tender, about 1 more hour. Remove the pan from the oven, and allow the shanks to cool in their cooking liquid.

4 Transfer the shanks to a plate or bowl, and strain the braising liquid through a fine-mesh strainer into a saucepan; discard the solids. Bring the braising liquid to a simmer over medium-high heat. Skim the fat as it rises. (Alternatively, chill the sauce so the fat hardens on top and can be removed.) Reduce the braising liquid to about 2 cups (480 ml) of sauce, approximately 15 minutes. Season the sauce with salt and pepper to taste. Return the shanks to the cooking pan. Pour the sauce over the shanks, and reheat in the oven, basting with sauce frequently. Serve the shanks on a platter or in large bowls topped with sauce. Pair with a creamy risotto and an assortment of fresh seasonal vegetables on the side, if you like.

APPENDIXES

RECIPE INDEX

Meat & Eggs

Baked Eggs with Ratatouille,
Eric Ripert,134

Big Brined Herby Turkey,
Anne Burrell, 49

Braised Lamb Shanks,
Geoffrey Zakarian, 187

Classic Georgian "Pressed" Chicken
with Walnut and Beet Sauces,
Cindy Pawlcyn, 126

Chicken Stewed in Garlic and
Cinnamon (Kota Kapama),
Cat Cora, 67

Collards and Kimchi,
Edward Lee, 103

Family Meatballs with Tomatoes
and Peas, Marcella Hazan, 81

Helga's Meatballs with Lingonberry
Preserves and Quick Pickled Cucumbers, Marcus Samuelsson, 139

Huevos a la Cubana, José Andrés, 25

Potato Mushroom Cake,
Vitaly Paley, 123

Short Ribs Miroton, Daniel Boulud, 41

Zesty Holiday Deviled Eggs.
Sandra Lee, 106

Pasta & Grains

Arroz con Pollo, Ingrid Hoffmann, 84

Bucatini all'Amatriciana,
Mario Batali, 33

Classic Steamed Couscous,
Mourad Lahlou, 95

Eight-Treasure Rice, Ming Tsai, 173

Sopa Seca, Aarón Sánchez, 143

Seafood

Grilled Lobster with Sweet Corn
Butter and Bacon Marmalade,
Curtis Stone, 162

Fulton Fish Market Cioppino,
Bobby Flay, 75

Leigh-on-Sea Sole, Jamie Oliver, 118

Shrimp Clemenceau, Leah Chase, 58

Soupe de Poisson,
Anthony Bourdain, 45

Soups & Salads

Autumn Beet Salad with Spiced
Pecans, Pears, and Fourme D'Ambert,
Frank Stitt, 159

Caramelized Plantain Soup with
Smoked Ham and Sour Cream,
Norman Van Aken, 179

Chicken Soup, Tom Colicchio, 61

Fall Salad of Cauliflower, Butter
Lettuce, Brussels, Radish, Currants,
and Carrot with Cider Vinaigrette,
Hugh Acheson, 21

Fuji Apple Salad Kimchi, Smoked
Jowl, and Maple Labne,
David Chang, 55

New-Style Caldo Verde,
Emeril Lagasse, 89

Sweets

Chestnut Jam, Marc Murphy, 114

Mother's Linzer Cookies,
Wolfgang Puck, 130

Swedish Pancakes,
Paul Berglund, 37

Vegetarian

Avocado Banana-Chaat,
Vikram Sunderam, 167

Birbal Kee Khitcheree, Suvir Saran, 149

Fava Bean Falafel, Michael Mina, 111

Green Mango Curry
Padma Lakshmi, 98

Grilled Corn on the Cob,
Alice Waters, 183

Hummus-Masbacha,
Michael Solomonov, 155

Vegetable Parmesan,
Giada de Laurentiis, 71

Zucchini Fritters,
Donatella Arpaia, 29

191

CONVERSIONS

Volume

¼ teaspoon	1.2 milliliters
½ teaspoon	2.5 milliliters
1 teaspoon	5 milliliters
1 tablespoon	15 milliliters
¼ cup	60 milliliters
⅓ cup	80 milliliters
½ cup	120 milliliters
⅔ cup	160 milliliters
¾ cup	175 milliliters
1 cup	240 milliliters

Mass

4 ounces	110 grams
8 ounces	224 grams
12 ounces	340 grams
16 ounces	455 grams

Temperature

FAHRENHEIT	CELSIUS
350 degrees	180 degrees
375 degrees	190 degrees
400 degrees	200 degrees
425 degrees	220 degrees

Length

⅛ inch	0.3 centimeter
¼ inch	0.6 centimeter
½ inch	1.25 centimeter
1 inch	2.5 centimeter
2 inches	5 centimeters
6 inches	15 centimeters
9 inches	23 centimeters
9 x 13 inches	23 x 33 centimeters
12 inches	30.5 centimeters

CREDITS

Page 4: Photograph © Sarah Morgan Karp

Page 5: Photographs © Rinne Allen (top); © Will Blunt, starchefs.com (bottom)

Page 6: Photograph © Grant Cornett (second from top)

Page 7: Photographs (second and third from top) © Sarah Morgan Karp

Page 10: Photograph © Sarah Morgan Karp

Page 12: Photograph © Sarah Morgan Karp

Page 14: Photograph © Sarah Morgan Karp

Page 22: Photograph © Aaron Clamage

Page 27: Photograph © Marissa Scarna

Page 29: Recipe reproduced from *Donatella Cooks: Simple Food Made Glamorous* by Donatella Arpaia, 2012, Rodale

Page 30: Photographs © kengoodmanphotography.com (top), © Quentin Bacon (bottom)

Page 33: Recipe reproduced from *Molto Italiano: 327 Simple Italian Recipes to Cook at Home* by Mario Batali, 2005, Ecco

Page 38: Photograph © Thomas Schauer

Page 41: Recipe reproduced from *Daniel Boulud's Café Boulud Cookbook* by Daniel Boulud, 1999, Scribner

Page 42: Photograph © CNN

Page 49-50: Recipe reproduced from *Own Your Kitchen: Recipes to Inspire and Empower* by Anne Burrell, 2013, Clarkson Potter

Page 51: Photograph © Quentin Bacon, reprinted from *Own Your Kitchen* courtesy of Clarkson Potter

Page 52-53: Photographs © Gabrielle Stabile

Page 55: Recipe reproduced from *Momofuku* by David Chang and Peter Meehan, 2009, Clarkson Potter, a division of Random House Inc.;

Page 58: Recipe reproduced from *The Dooky Chase Cookbook* by Leah Chase, 1990, Pelican Publishing

Page 60: Photograph © Bill Bettencourt

Page 61: Recipe by Tom Colicchio, *Chef on a Shoestring,* CBSNews, New York, December 2000

Page 62: Photograph © Lucy Lean, ladlesandjellyspoons.com

Page 67: Recipe courtesy of Cat Cora, catcora.com.

Page 68: Photograph © 2011 Amy Neunsinger

Page 71: Recipe by Giada de Laurentiis, from *Giada at Home,* Food Network, Los Angeles, September 2009

Page 75-76: Recipe by Bobby Flay, from *Throwdown! with Bobby Flay,* Food Network, New York, January 2009

Page 81: Recipe reproduced from *Hazan Family Favorites* by Giuliano Hazan, 2012, Stewart, Tabori & Chang

Page 82: Photograph © Andrew Meade

Page 84-86: Recipe by Ingrid Hoffmann, *Simply Delicioso with Ingrid Hoffmann,* Food Network, New York, August 2007

Page 88: Photograph © Steven Freeman 2013

Page 89: Recipe by Emeril Lagasse, from *EMERIL 20-40-60: Fresh Food Fast,* HarperStudio, New York, 2009, courtesy of Martha Stewart Living Omnimedia, Inc.

Page 90: Photograph © Steven Freeman 2009

Page 92: Photographs © Deborah Jones

Page 95-96: Recipe reproduced from *Mourad: New Moroccan* by Mourad Lahlou, 2011, Artisan

Page 98: Recipe reproduced from *Tangy Tart Hot & Sweet: A World of Recipes for Every Day* by Padma Lakshmi, 2007, Weinstein Books

Page 98: Photograph © Charles Thompson

Page 103: Recipe reproduced from *Smoke & Pickles* by Edward Lee, 2013, Artisan

Page 104: Photograph © Ben Fink Photography

Page 106: Recipe from *Every Dish Delivers: 365 Days of Fast, Fresh, Affordable Meals* by Sandra Lee, 2013, Hyperion

Page 108: Photograph © 2011 Lindsay Borden

Page 111: Recipe by Michael Mina, cooktasteeat.com/dish/fava-bean-falafel

Page 116: Photograph © 2008-2009 David Loftus and Chris Terry

Page 118: from *Jamie Oliver's Great Britain* by Jamie Oliver, 2012, Hyperion

Page 119: Photograph © 2008-2009 David Loftus and Chris Terry

Page 120: Photograph © John Valis

Page 123: Recipe reproduced from *The Paley's Place Cookbook: Recipes and Stories from the Pacific Northwest* by Vitaly Paley and Kimberly Paley, 2008, Ten Speed Press

Page 124: Photograph © Alex Farnum

Page 126-127: Recipe from *CINDY'S SUPPER CLUB* by Cindy Pawlcyn, copyright ©2012 by Cynthia Lynn Pawlcyn. Reprinted by permission of Ten Speed Press, an imprint of the Crown Publishing Group, a division of Random House LLC

Page 128: Photograph © Greg Gorman

Page 130-131: Recipe reproduced from *Wolfgang Puck Makes It Easy* by Wolfgang Puck, 2004, Rutledge Hill Press

Page 132: Photograph © Nigel Parry

Page 134: Recipe by Eric Ripert, aveceric.com/baked-eggs-with-ratatouille

Page 139-140: Recipe by Marcus Samuelsson, *Good Morning America,* ABC News, December 2011

Page 143: Recipe from *Simple Food, Big Flavor: Unforgettable Mexican-Inspired Recipes from My Kitchen to Yours* by Aarón Sánchez, Michael Harlan Turkell, and JJ Goode, 2011, Atria

Page 146: Photograph © Jim Franco

Page 148: Photograph © Ben Fink

Page 149-151: Recipe reproduced from *Masala Farm: Stories and Recipes from an Uncommon Life in the Country* by Suvir Saran, Raquel Pelzel, and Charlie Burd, 2011, Chronicle

Page 155: Recipe by Michael Solomonov, *Food Network Specials: Food Revolution,* Food Network, 2011

Page 159-160: Recipe reproduced from *Frank Stitt's Southern Table* by Frank Stitt, Christopher Hirsheimer, and Pat Conroy, 2004, Artisan

Page 164-165: Recipe reproduced from *What's for Dinner? Delicious Recipes for a Busy Life* by Curtis Stone, 2013, Ballantine

Page 170: © WGBH/Anthony Tieuli

Page 173: Recipe reproduced from *Simply Ming in Your Kitchen: 80 Recipes to Watch, Learn, Cook & Enjoy* by Ming Tsai with Arthur Boehm, 2012, Kyle

Page 174: Recipe reproduced from *Simply Ming One-Pot Meals* by Ming Tsai, 2010, Kyle

Page 175: Photograph © Bill Bettencourt

Page 176-179: Photographs © Penny de Los Santos

Page 179: Recipe reproduced from *My Key West Kitchen,* published by Kyle BooksPage 180: Photograph © Gilles Mingasson

Page 183: Recipe reproduced from *Chez Panisse Vegetables* by Alice Waters, 1996, HarperCollins

Page 187: Recipe reproduced from *Geoffrey Zakarian's Town/Country: 150 Recipes for Life Around the Table* by Geoffrey Zakarian, 2006, Clarkson Potter

Page 190: Photograph © Sarah Morgan Karp

Page 192: Photograph © Sarah Morgan Karp

Page 199: Photograph © Sarah Morgan Karp.

INDEX

ACKNOWLEDGMENTS

Deepest gratitude to:

My amazing husband, who inspires me to pay attention to the details.

My brilliant mother, for the brilliant title.

Kate Meyers and Scott Mowbray, for their wisdom, talent and generosity.

Marta Hallett, for her gentle but firm guidance throughout.

To the enthusiasm & unreserved support of:

All of the extraordinary chefs!

And,

Alicia Ybarbo
Andrea Masterson
Andy Cohen
Ann Loftus
Antoinette Machiaverna
Bill Brand
Brian Meyers
Bryant
Bradley
Jillian and Will
Caryl Stern
Dad
Deb Shriver
Debbie Kosofsky
Debby Stevens and family
Deborah and Allen Grubman
Eden Fesehaye
Ellen Levine
Jeannette Park
Jessica Guerrero
Trevor Quinlan and family
Lucy Lean
Mindy Grossman
Pamela Fiori
Sarah Morgan Karp
Victoria Brody